PARAGON ISSUES IN PHILOSOPHY

PARAGON ISSUES IN PHILOSOPHY

African Philosophy: The Essential Readings
Tsenay Serequeberhan, Editor
Critical Theory and Philosophy
David Ingram
Critical Theory: The Essential Readings
David Ingram and Julia Simon-lngram, Editors
Foundations of Cognitive Science: The Essential Readings
Jay L. Garfield, Editor
Foundations of Philosophy of Science: Recent Developments
James H. Fetzer, Editor
Living the Good Life: An Introduction to Moral Philosophy
Gordon Graham
Meaning and Truth: Essential Readings in Modern Semantics
Jay L. Garfield and Murray Kiteley, Editors
Metaphysics: A Contemporary Introduction
John Post
Philosophy and Feminist Criticism: An Introduction
Eve BrowningCole
Philosophy and Cognitive Science
James H. Fetzer
Philosophy of Science
James H. Fetzer
Philosophy of Sex and Love: An Introduction
Alan Soble
Philosophy of Sport
Drew Hyland
Philosophy of Technology: An Introduction
Don Ihde
Problems in Personal Identity
James Baillie
Self-Interest and Beyond
David Holley
Social and Political Philosophy
William McBride
Woman and the History of Philosophy
Nancy Tuana

THE PARAGON ISSUES IN PHILOSOPHY SERIES

At colleges and universities, interest in the traditional areas of philosophy remains strong. Many new currents flow within them, too, but some of these—the rise of cognitive science, for example, or feminist philosophy—went largely unnoticed in undergraduate philosophy courses until the end of the 1980s. The Paragon Issues in Philosophy Series responds to both perennial and newly influential concerns by bringing together a team of able philosophers to address the fundamental issues in philosophy today and to outline the state of contemporary discussion about them.

More than twenty volumes are scheduled; they are organized into three major categories. The first covers the standard topics—metaphysics, theory of knowledge, ethics, and political philosophy—stressing innovative developments in those disciplines. The second focuses on more specialized but still vital concerns in the philosophies of science, religion, history, sport, and other areas. The third category explores new work that relates philosophy and fields such as feminist criticism, medicine, economics, technology, and literature.

The level of writing is aimed at undergraduate students who have little previous experience studying philosophy. The books provide brief but accurate introductions that appraise the state of the art in their fields and show how the history of thought about their topics developed. Each volume is complete in itself but also complements others in the series.

Traumatic change characterizes these last years of the twentieth century: all of it involves philosophical issues. The editorial staff at Paragon house has worked with us to develop this series. We hope it will encourage the understanding needed in our times, which are as complicated and problematic as they are promising.

John K. Roth
Claremont McKenna College

Frederick Sontag
Pomona College

SELF-INTEREST AND BEYOND

DAVID M. HOLLEY

SELF-INTEREST AND BEYOND

PARAGON HOUSE ✦ ST. PAUL

First Edition 1999

Published in the United States by
Paragon House
2700 University Avenue West
St. Paul, MN 55114

Copyright © 1999 by David M. Holley

All rights reserved. No part of this book may be reproduced, in any form, without written permission from the publisher, unless by a reviewer who wishes to quote brief passages.

Library of Congress Cataloging-in-Publication Data

Holley, David M., 1948-
Self-interest and beyond / David M. Holley. — 1st ed.
p. cm. — (Paragon issues in philosophy)
Includes bibliographical references and index.
ISBN 1-55778-778-6 (alk. paper)
1. Self-interest. I Title. II. Series.
BJ1474.H64 1999
171'.9—dc21 99-17823
CIP

Manufactured in the United States of America

10 9 8 7 6 5 4 3 2 1

For current information about all releases from Paragon House, visit the web site at http://www.paragonhouse.com

For my parents

Oscar M. Holley and Dorothy A. Holley

CONTENTS

PREFACE

This book is not written for professional philosophers, though I think there is much here to interest them. My intended audience, however, is composed of readers without formal philosophical training who are willing to do some serious reflection about their lives. Although my topic bears some resemblance to issues raised in self-help books, this work requires considerably more attention and effort than books of that genre. I am trying to engage the reader in the kind of thinking that classical and contemporary philosophers have done about how to live.

In our age self-interest has become a way of thinking that powerfully influences how we shape our lives. For many people it is the default mode for all their practical reasoning. Often when that mode is engaged, it threatens to overwhelm any consideration that does not fit within its strictures. I am attempting to show how to give self-interested thinking its due, while enlarging our field of awareness to include factors besides self-interest. By putting this mode of thought in an appropriate context, I try to show how it can be less superficial than it usually is and more useful in helping us achieve the kinds of lives we want.

Because I am writing primarily to people who are not specialists in philosophy, I have refrained from exploring some issues of philosophical interest in much depth. I have also limited my use of the kind of technical precision and systematic analysis that is often helpful in philosophic work. Sometimes I was unable to keep myself from touching on issues that may be of only minimal interest to the general reader, but my main concern has been to write the kind of book that would be stimulating and helpful to intelligent readers who want to think in greater depth about their lives.

I would like to thank my colleagues at the University of Southern Mississippi who have read portions of the manuscript. These have included Jeanne Ezell, Jim Hollandsworth, Susan Malone, Kate Greene, Jameela Lares, and Forrest Wood. Thanks also to Melissa Iverson for many helpful suggestions. As much as I would like to blame someone else for the work's deficiencies, I am afraid that I will have to accept that responsibility myself.

Introduction

SELF-INTERESTED THINKING

Imagine that you are having one of those anxiety dreams that are very common among college students. It's the last week of the semester, and suddenly you realize that you have forgotten to attend one of the classes you signed up for. It's too late to drop, and you have to take the final exam totally unprepared. You are in a state of near panic when you pick up the exam and read the only question: "If you had to live your life over again, what would you do differently?" You aren't sure what the course is. You think that perhaps it might be a philosophy course. As you are trying to figure this out, you wake up with the question still on your mind.

Experience is said to be a good teacher, and, like most of us, you believe that you have learned some things from experience. So you think to yourself that if you had your life to live over, you would eliminate the mistakes you have made. You wouldn't be so naive as to drift into that manipulative relationship. You would work harder at developing your musical talent. You would pay more attention to your diet before your weight problem got out of control. However, there is a problem in imagining actually making these changes. You have to imagine yourself with a knowledge and discipline that you apparently did not have at the time, for otherwise what is to prevent you from making the same mistakes? But if you are different in those ways, how did you get to be different? Did you learn what you needed from some source other than experience or develop your discipline by some means other than practice? If you imagine yourself knowing in advance all the consequences of all your mistakes, your godlike knowledge makes the person living the life too different from an actual human being. You have to imagine yourself as having greater insight and better skills of self-management in order to picture a possible improvement, but you need to imagine those differences as having some plausible connection with the life you actually live.

However, if this thought experiment allows you to imagine yourself being different, you realize that you haven't been nearly radical enough. You shouldn't just think about altering unfortunate decisions or following through on lapsed resolutions. You need to imagine the possibility of developing your capacities in entirely different ways. There are many possible selves that you could have become, and you have by your choices shaped yourself in a particular way. By repeated choices you have formed habits of thinking and feeling that have become second nature to you. You have cultivated some concerns and let others wither and die. If you were given the chance to live your life over, you could become a different person, but then you would need to decide what kind of person to become.

You do not have the option of living your life over, but you do have some control over your future life. You can certainly try not to make the same kinds of mistakes you have made in the past, and you can make some effort to do the things you now recognize as worthwhile. But you also have in your power a capacity which you may not fully appreciate: the capacity to shape the self that you will become in the future. It is easy to think of your self as a fixed quantity that you can take for granted, and admittedly, all of us tend to settle into habitual patterns of thinking and acting much of the time. However, you can either acquiesce to the pulls of your inclinations and allow your self to solidify into an unchangeable substance, or you can take steps to become something different from what you are. Taking seriously your power over the future means taking seriously the possible alternative selves and alternative lives that you might try to develop.

This is difficult to do. When we engage in practical decision-making, it is relatively easy to focus on how a particular course of action might produce a result we would like or help us to avoid some result we would dislike. However, it is possible for something to seem attractive to the kind of self I am now and yet hinder my efforts to shape my self in a desired direction. I might aspire to become a world-class scholar, yet find the daily activities of an intellectual dabbler much more to my present liking. If I am interested in building a preferred kind of life, I need to discover how to create the kind of self able to live that life. Unfortunately, one of the most troublesome obstacles to creating such a self may be produced by my own patterns of thinking.

THE SELF-INTERESTED POINT OF VIEW

There is a way of thinking about how to live that exercises a captivating influence on us. It is what I will call the self-interested point of view. A person assumes this viewpoint when she evaluates potential actions in terms of what gains or losses they are likely to produce for her. All of us recognize the possibility of receiving something of personal benefit or avoiding a personal setback as reasons for action. When a person takes the self-interested point of view, she weighs the expected positive and negative consequences of her actions in an attempt to discover which way of acting is likely to benefit her most.

To the person who has become accustomed to thinking in self-interested fashion, virtually any aspect of life becomes susceptible to this sort of evaluation. Decisions about whether to start a romantic relationship, to have children, to develop an appreciation for poetry, or to run for the school board can all be analyzed in terms of what benefits the proposed behavior is expected to produce. From the point of view of self-interest, the relevant questions in any situation are always, "What can I get for myself?" and "What would I have to risk?"

While this way of thinking comes easily to us, its conclusions can be problematic. Unless we are careful, our efforts to evaluate potential actions in terms of personal gains and losses can defeat our purposes in living the kind of life we want. This is not just because self-interested calculations tend to be shortsighted, failing to take into account potential long-term gains and losses (though shortsightedness is a problem). It is because our judgment of what benefits to seek or what losses to avoid presupposes a judgment about what kind of self it is desirable to be. We may be extremely effective at determining how to maximize gains and minimize losses, but if the gains and losses are measured in relation to a self we could not aspire to become, we are engaging in a kind of self-interested thinking which has lost contact with the point of pursuing self-interest.

Suppose, for example, that a public official has the opportunity to receive a large sum of money in exchange for favored treatment of a constituent. Imagine that the favoritism is unlikely to be detected by others and that there is every indication that the monetary transaction can be kept secret. Is it in the official's self-interest to take the money? Some would answer yes, suggesting that this is a case where self-interest conflicts with doing the morally right action. However, judging the action of taking the bribe as self-interested requires us to consider the nature of the self receiving the benefit. If we imagine a person who lacks fundamental moral principles forbidding such acts, we can imagine that under the right circumstances, receiving the money would be a reasonable risk to obtain a personal benefit. But what if we imagine a person who has internalized a fundamental principle against betraying the public trust by taking bribes? Is it in the self-interest of *that* individual to take the money? Can we determine what is in a person's self-interest without considering that some acts might be a betrayal of the self whose interest is being sought?

THINKING ABOUT YOUR SELF

The trouble with much of what passes for self-interested thinking is that it contains little, if any, consideration of the self. We ask, "What can I get?" or "What would I have to give up?" but omit from our reflection the *I* who is to be getting or giving something up. This omission might seem to be unimportant, except for the fact that the point of pursuing self-interest is to benefit a particular self, not just any self, and the fact that something might be in the interest of some other self does not show whether it is in *my* interest. To judge that, I have to consider what kinds of concerns I regard as fundamental to my identity and what constraints I recognize as binding on the pursuit of my goals.

Even that is not enough. As I try to bring the self into the reflective mix, I need to consider not just the self I am now, but the aspirations I have for myself. I may not be a very loving person now, but if I have an image of my ideal self as loving, it might be important for me to maintain that ideal as a real possibility. However, my behavior can make it unrealistic even to aspire to this ideal by creating habits which are too difficult to overcome or by altering my interests and concerns. While I can change my ideal for myself, I cannot always do so without loss, and in some cases what I am in danger of losing is my self-respect.

The potential loss of a self-concept on which someone's self-respect rests is not a loss to be weighed against other sorts of losses. Thinking about it that way fails to take into account how any other gain or loss presupposes the self. Yet some potential changes amount to losing the self. Surprisingly, such a change may not even be detected. Kierkegaard observes, "The greatest hazard of all, losing the self, can occur very quietly in the world, as if it were nothing at all. No other loss can occur so quietly; any other loss—an arm, a leg, five dollars, a wife, etc.—is sure to be noticed."[1]

So a serious effort to do self-interested thinking calls for something less superficial than the weighing of obvious gains and losses. It calls for examination of whether the self that is needed to seek certain types of gains or avoid certain types of losses is a self I would be willing to become. If I could not be satisfied with becoming a deceptive and manipulative person, then the successes I could achieve by pursuing policies of deception and manipulation should not convince me that pursuing such policies is in my interest. The question of what a particular mode of life will do to me is crucial to determining whether it is in my interest to live that kind of life.

Furthermore, the capacities I have to receive certain types of benefits depend on the kind of self I develop. Suppose I approach each relationship with the idea that I will get as much personal benefit as I can from the relationship. I only value the other person as a means to my goal of getting satisfaction. I am ready to pull out of the relationship whenever it becomes apparent that I am giving more than I am getting. It is fairly clear that this calculating mode of thought will effectively close me off from certain kinds of benefits that others find in relationships. The joys of friendship or love are only fully available for the person who is able to value other people for their own sakes, and not merely for the sake of benefits they can provide. Getting the benefits of love presupposes that you are the kind of person who is able to give and receive love.

TRANSCENDING SELF-INTERESTED THINKING

This book is an attempt to show that self-interested thinking, when carried far enough, involves us in a different kind of thinking: reflection about what kind of self to be. Reflection on the self furnishes a context necessary for making reasonable judgments of self-interest. Without such a context, the role of these judgments in our lives would be obscure. Seeking to get as much benefit as possible, while ignoring the self whose benefit is sought, can be done only if a self is implicitly assumed, and this exercise is self-defeating when the assumed self is incapable of living the kind of life a person seeks to have.

However, when we think about our self-interest in the context of our aspirations for the self, we may discover that there is room in our lives for motivations other than self-interest. These motivations are activated, not by competing with self-interested reasons for action, but as expressions of what the self is concerned about. For example, if I aspire to be a person who lives a meaningful life, I am unlikely to do so without developing a variety of concerns which are not self-interested in any direct sense. Suppose, for instance, that I become interested in scientific research. Even if I were to develop this interest in a calculated attempt to make my life more meaningful (which is unlikely), the interest flourishes only if it takes on a life of its own. When it becomes part of me, I pursue it, not because it is a means to achieve some benefit for myself, but because it expresses one of my deepest concerns. Having concerns like this for things outside of myself pulls me away from a life that is preoccupied with my own benefit.

Preoccupation of the self with its benefits is what Robert Bellah and his coauthors in *Habits of the Heart* describe as a kind of individualistic trap that a person can fall into. Suggesting what they think is a hopeful sign for American culture, they write, "...few have found life devoted to 'personal ambition and consumerism' satisfactory, and most are seeking in one way or another to transcend the limitations of a self-centered life."[2] If pursuing the preferences of a self that is narrowly focused on its own satisfaction leaves a person with a sense of emptiness, it is in part because the self whose interests are being promoted seems hardly worth the energy. A fuller life requires a more substantial self.

Building a more substantial self involves developing concerns that extend beyond the confines of an individual life. A self that is wrapped up in efforts to get all it can is a shallow and isolated entity. To acquire greater depth, we must internalize concerns for enterprises that connect us with something larger than the self. Paradoxically, we achieve greater individuality when we incorporate into the self the kinds of concerns that can shift our attention and energy away from the self. Self-centeredness is overcome, not by giving up interest in the self, but by becoming self-interested in a different way, interested in developing the kind of self with enough substance to live a satisfying life.

Far from being a secure possession that can be taken for granted and ignored, the self is an achievement which must be carefully nurtured and protected. In one sense having a self is the easiest thing in the world, but becoming the kind of self capable of living a fulfilling and meaningful life can be a complex and arduous undertaking, requiring a substantial amount of self-knowledge and self-control. It is unrealistic to expect such a self to emerge by accident or by a policy of following one's strongest desire.

The intelligent way to pursue our self-interest is to allow our reflection on possible gains and losses to be regulated by reflection on what kind of self we aspire to be and how our actions are contributing to building such a self. When this kind of reflection leads us to form a self that is concerned about a variety of things other than its own interest, we might say that our self-interested thinking has moved beyond self-interest. Typically when self-interested thinking fails to advance beyond self-interest, it is because we stop it at a point that is inadequate for our purposes in using such thinking. It is easy to imagine that we are pursuing our interests when our attention is captured by powerful attractions. However, when we place our self-interested thinking in service of building a desirable life, we put the pursuit of self-interest in proper perspective. From this point of view it becomes clear that the only interests worth pursuing are those belonging to a self that is worth having.

Part One

THE PURSUIT OF SELF-INTEREST

Because people are creatures of habit, time eventually leaves a person with the accumulation of dispositions that we think of as a character...when it comes to sorting out what is in our self-interest, we are relatively inept in situations where what is at stake is our character. (David Schmidtz[1])

We do not just look from an act outwards, towards its further and further consequences...we should also look from the whole of life inwards, to find the acts that give it its general contours. This means abandoning the narrow perspective that sees acts as making ripples, some of which admittedly last for a long while.... Some of our most important acts are not like that; they are important because they alter the character of deliberation; they regulate act-by-act deliberation to a relatively small segment of life. (James Griffin[2])

PRELUDE TO PART ONE

Almost everyone is familiar with how shortsightedness can keep us from acting in our interest. We feel the allure of some immediate benefit, but fail to take into account the likely negative consequences. Sometimes this kind of shortsightedness results in suffering we could have avoided had we taken a long-enough view. The effective pursuit of self-interest surely means overcoming the human tendency to focus on short-term consequences while minimizing the long-term results. However, becoming adept at seeing what results we may expect in the long-run is not sufficient, for we may still defeat our purposes by evaluating this broader range of consequences in a misguided fashion. When we assume that we can weigh potential gains or losses without giving much consideration to the self who is to receive the gains or suffer the losses, we run the risk of distorting our evaluations in several ways.

First, the self is not a constant. While we may be aware of a wide range of potential consequences of our actions, we find it very difficult to recognize that among the potential consequences are changes to the self. No single action looks as if it will greatly alter the self, and it is hard to take into account what kinds of effects will be produced by repeated actions. However, we can scarcely deny that the self is shaped by its actions. The ways we seek gains and try to avoid losses help to form a particular character, and maintaining the right kind of character can be crucial to receiving the kinds of gains we value most. Discounting the likely effects of our patterns of behavior on the self opens us to the risk of becoming the kind of person who lacks the capacities needed to live our preferred way of life.

A related problem is that failure to think about the self compromises our ability to measure gains and losses. We assume that we can look at individual results, labeling them as positive or negative in themselves. However, the question of whether something is a benefit for us depends on how it fits into the kind of life we want to live. Something that might seem desirable in itself (e.g., experiencing sexual pleasure from an extra-marital affair) might be inconsistent with a self-conception (e.g., being a faithful spouse) that forms an indispensable component of the life someone wants to build. Assessing the value of an experience is not just a matter of thinking in a long-term way. We need to assess the value of potential gains or losses in relation to a reflectively-chosen conception of a desirable life. The importance of particular pluses and minuses is indeterminate unless we are able to give them a place in a general conception of the life we want to have and the kind of self we want to be.

Part One attempts to show how a serious effort to think about our self-interest calls for reflection on what kind of self to be.

Chapter One, for example, makes clear that consistently acting in one's own interest requires the cultivation of capacities for reflective judgment and self-management. All of us are tempted to follow various unreflective impulses, but it is only by becoming a disciplined and reflective person that we can effectively pursue our self-interest. So it is important to consider how our patterns of action contribute to or erode our abilities to coordinate and control our impulses.

Chapter Two responds to a widespread confusion about human motivation: the idea that we are capable of being motivated only by self-interested concerns. When we understand that it is possible to build into the self a variety of motivating concerns, we can expand our awareness of our potential control over the self. Achieving the life we want requires us to develop the motivations appropriate to that mode of life, and this calls for discerning what pattern of actions is likely to alter the self's motivational structure in the desired way.

Chapter Three begins with a simple conception of self-interest as getting what we want. When we think of our self-interest in this way, it is fairly clear that we must prioritize our wants. The most appealing way of prioritizing is to evaluate particular wants from the perspective of what we want for our lives as a whole. Our conception of a desirable life may be modified in the light of experience and reflection, but it provides us a way of determining whether satisfying particular wants promotes our interest or not. Furthermore, any conception of a desirable life will imply some conception of a self able to live that life. So in seeking the kind of life we want, we need to determine what kind of self is needed and how we can produce and maintain such a self.

Chapter Four raises the problem of how to deal with unwanted things that are likely to come into our lives despite our best efforts. It becomes clear in this chapter that we need a conception of a desirable life that is flexible enough to include some undesirable elements. We also need the kind of self that is able to face up to the adversities of life and continue to live in accordance with its reflective values in difficult circumstances. To be effective, our thinking about self-interest needs to include reflection on how to become such a self.

Chapter One

THE DIFFICULTY OF SELF-INTERESTED BEHAVIOR

The thing to be lamented is not that men have so great regard to their own good, or interest in the present world, for they have not enough... (Joseph Butler[1])

...if you cannot control yourself, you will scarcely find anyone else who is able to do it. (Judge Wilhelm in Kierkegaard's *Either/Or*[2])

Telling people to be concerned about their self-interest sounds a little like reminding them to breathe. We may think that such advice is altogether superfluous, that acting in self-interested fashion is something we will do habitually and naturally. In fact, however, the effective pursuit of self-interest requires intellectual and emotional skills that are unlikely to develop by chance, but call for cultivation and practice. To consistently act in your own interest, you need to become the kind of person who possesses the character traits needed for self-interested behavior.

What leads us to assume that self-interested behavior is easy? Perhaps this idea has something to do with the fact that so much effort is required to train us to pay attention to the interests of others. Children are given instructions designed to alert them to be aware of the feelings of others and to respond with empathy:

"How would you like it if someone pulled your hair?" "When you speak to your little sister that way, it makes her sad." We may assume that instructions intended to make us fit for living with others are molding us away from our natural state of self-interest, that left without external pressures, we would diligently pursue our own good. But such an assumption rests on a confusion about what the pursuit of self-interest involves. An example may help to make this clear.

Suppose that John has suddenly begun to spend his spare time as a volunteer, building affordable housing for the poor. Imagine that people who know John are somewhat suspicious of his motives. He has never shown much interest in helping others up to now, much less people who are not in a position to benefit him in return. He must have some kind of hidden motivation, they think. Imagine that a little observation reveals a motivation that seems to fit better with John's past behavior. John has developed a strong attraction to Betty who spends much of her time doing this kind of work, and his volunteering allows him to be near Betty.

It is tempting to conclude that we now have an account of the change in John's behavior that shows it to be self-interested. However, drawing this conclusion on the basis of discovering a potential payoff for John conceals an important ambiguity. Some actions aimed at personal payoffs are self-interested in the sense of genuinely advancing a person's interest, but others are self-interested only in the sense of enabling the person to gain something he wants for himself.

John's attraction to Betty may well be a motivation for his behavior, but should we conclude that in acting on the basis of this attraction, John is pursuing his self-interest? There are any number of reasons why allowing his attraction to determine his behavior might be foolish from a self-interested point of view. Perhaps John knows on the basis of past experience that his attraction to Betty is obsessive and clearly not reciprocated. Perhaps his relationship with Betty resembles previous relationships which turned out to be needlessly self-destructive. Perhaps the time spent with Betty will interfere with the more promising relationship John now has with Sheila. Perhaps the attempt to gain Betty's attention will inevitably lead to a clash with Betty's husband.

We have no difficulty in understanding how someone might act on the basis of an attraction, but it is potentially misleading to lump together under a single heading actions which might range all the way from impulsive and ill-considered choices to choices reflecting informed judgments of personal benefit. A great many of the things we find ourselves pursuing are clearly not in our self-interest; we pursue them without considering what is good for us, or even with the realization that they are definitely not good for us. It would probably be best if we could reserve the label "self-interested behavior" for those actions that have some plausible connection with the person's good, but even if we do not, we can at least get clear that there is a world of difference between actions that aim at fulfilling an unreflective desire and actions that a person has good reason to believe are personally beneficial.

REFLECTIVE SELF-INTEREST

A classic discussion of human motivation, developed in an eighteenth-century collection of sermons by Joseph Butler, distinguishes between actions motivated by "self-love" and actions which are done for the "gratification of a present passion." While there are certainly cases in which the "cool and settled" judgments of self-love coincide with the concerns generated by particular passions, there are also instances when the two kinds of motivations are at odds with each other. Self-love sometimes requires a person to suppress or weaken a present desire which it is not in her interest to attempt to satisfy.

It is in the light of this distinction that Butler remarks, "The thing to be lamented is not that men have so great regard to their own good, or interest in the present world, for they have not enough..."[3] We might have expected a Christian preacher to take us to task for caring too much about ourselves and too little about others. While Butler does think our concern for others too weak, he is equally convinced that a strong concern for our own interests is something to be cultivated. We need both to care more about others and to care more about ourselves.

Butler's analysis reveals to us that our actions are motivated in a wide variety of ways. We may act to satisfy our curiosity, to achieve recognition, to show our boredom, or to relieve hunger. We may be motivated by jealousy or friendship or resentment or mercy. Whether or not allowing a particular motivation to be expressed in action will benefit us is a matter for judgment, and it is at this level that our capacity for self-love is apparent. Self-love involves a kind of reflective coordination of the particular impulses so as to achieve what is good for us overall. Sometimes self-love will affirm the satisfaction of a particular impulse, but allowing a free rein to our impulses would be evidence for Butler of having too little regard for ourselves. What we need is an intelligent ordering of our desires which allows us to pursue those impulses that are genuinely in our interest and reject those that are not. Clearly this requires both some facility at making judgments as well as internalized habits of control. Far from being easy and undemanding, the pursuit of self-interest involves a complex set of skills that are only acquired through diligent effort.

A genuinely self-interested person would have strong reason to develop and nurture the control over immediate inclination needed for self-interested action. Such control calls for bringing emotions and desires into conformity with reflective judgments of self-interest. Forming a self capable of this sort of inner harmony is not an easy task, but neglecting this kind of self-formation can result in a self that is not fully able to act in its own interest. It is only by acquiring adequate habits of self-control that we can expect to consistently follow our judgment of what is good for us.

SELF-DESTRUCTIVE BEHAVIOR

People have an amazing capacity to disregard their own interest. Michael Ryan has given an autobiographical account of how he continued to follow patterns of behavior that he knew were not good for him. Ryan had achieved an enviable position in the world. His poetry had won critical acclaim. He held a prestigious position at Princeton University. But after repeated cases of seducing female students, he was fired from his job. Despite this setback, Ryan continued the same pattern of behavior, destroying two marriages in the process. He writes that his sexual obsession

> determined what I thought and what I felt. My personality was formed around it. All of my talents, all my good qualities as a human being were devoted to serving it, and I was willing to sacrifice anything to do it. Although I could perform practical tasks perfectly well, it was ruining my life, and had been for a long time.[4]

What was ruining Ryan's life was in one sense his own choices. But the addictive quality suggested by his account makes us wonder whether we should even call his actions choices. Something clearly went wrong in his capacity to live the kind of life he would reflectively want for himself. We may be inclined to think of his situation as pathological, needing some kind of cure. But the difference between this kind of pathology and more ordinary failures of control appears to be a matter of degree. Our newspapers regularly give us accounts of apparently ordinary decent people who act in ways that risk the destruction of what they care about most. People can often look back at their own behavior with a kind of amazement: How could I have been so stupid? Even more startling, an individual can often realize retrospectively that at some level he knew that what he was doing was foolish and potentially disastrous. Sometimes it almost seems as if we deliberately sabotage ourselves.

Sara was a person of remarkable intellectual ability and social skills. She had been told many times that she had the ability to do whatever she wanted. People invariably saw in her an impressive potential. However, Sara found it difficult to actually settle on any long-term goals. She drifted through high school, making good grades with little effort. In college she did what she had to do to get by, changing her major whenever she found a subject challenging and settling on a major that was easy to finish. At no point did Sara invest much of herself in her studies. Relying on her raw talent, she was able to hold herself aloof from her education and resist any kind of thinking which would require too much of her.

After college Sara got married. She still couldn't decide what she wanted to do with her life. It was as if committing herself to a course of action would rule out so many other good possibilities. Often she simply decided not to decide; the decision about whether to have children was so overwhelming that she repeatedly put it off until things were more settled. She held a number of low-level jobs, resisting any opportunities that would call for a significant amount of responsibility. With her husband's support Sara decided to go to graduate school. Though she impressed her teachers with her obvious ability, she sabotaged herself by refusing to turn in any work that could not meet her unrealistic perfectionistic standards.

Confused by her failure and unhappy with her life, Sara decided that her problem was her husband. She couldn't put her finger on any real fault, but he wasn't meeting her needs. She began to feel an attraction to another man, and saw him as just what she needed to feel good about herself again. Though she knew that the man had a history of marital infidelity, that his ex-wife claimed he was an alcoholic, and that by his own admission he had behaved in verbally abusive and controlling fashion, she was "in love" and convinced herself that he would change. She left her husband and married this man who she was sure would make her life complete.

While Sara might have acknowledged that some of her choices were foolish, she did not fully recognize the extent of her captivity to self-destructive impulses. She could have given plausible explanations for the choices she made, and she projected the image of one in control. But the inclinations governing these choices were rooted in patterns that had taken a firm hold in the distant past, and despite some struggles, she displayed an unfortunate inability to use her reflective judgment to rise above her inclinations and modify them into greater harmony with her goals. Increasingly susceptible to self-deceptive justifications, she clung to habits that ultimately compromised her ability to act in her own interest.

It is much easier to see self-destructive patterns of thinking and acting in others than to see them in ourselves. Sometimes we can convince ourselves that our problems are a result of not getting the right breaks or of having to deal with difficult people or other external factors. We tell ourselves that we did the best we could under the circumstances. It is not easy to look within and find that many of our difficulties are our own creation. We nurture habits which make us into people who lack the inner strength to face difficult challenges. Seeking the easy escape in the short run, we choose for ourselves paths which assure us of greater pain and suffering in the long run. By avoiding the difficult and demanding task of developing a self able to withstand the pressures and temptations we inevitably face, we leave ourselves vulnerable to patterns of rationalization and self-deception that support our self-destructive tendencies.

SKILLS OF SELF-MANAGEMENT

While there is no foolproof method for avoiding all self-destructive patterns of behavior, there are certain skills that enable a person to exercise control over impulses opposed to self-interest.[5] Developing these skills involves internalizing habits of thought and feeling as well as applying conscious strategies for managing recalcitrant impulses. We sometimes say that the person who uses skills of this sort possesses willpower or discipline or self-control. These labels are all ways of describing the ability to make our actions subject to our judgment rather than to some unreflective impulse.

Some of the impulses in need of control are desires for particular objects. The desire to place a bet or to show-off by taking unnecessary risks or to stay in bed rather than facing a day at the office might be very strong. An individual can recognize that acting in accordance with the desire is not in his best interest. But recognizing what is good for you and acting to achieve it are two different things. Sometimes philosophers have puzzled over whether the person who acts against his own judgment really *knows* that what he is doing is not good for him. Socrates apparently thought that a failure to do what is good was always a failure of knowledge. However, unless we resort to a specialized use of the term "knowledge," it is pretty clear that people do knowingly act against their better judgment. A man can realize that it is unwise to bet his whole paycheck or to continue smoking cigarettes or to put off repairing the roof, yet do it anyway.

Cases like these suggest the need for resisting some of our impulses. However, a person may get to the point where resistance has become very difficult, or even impossible. While at some earlier point, the individual might have developed industrious work habits, years of sloth may have created invisible bonds, making any resolutions ineffectual. It is probably good strategy for a person to tell herself that it is never too late, but when we have failed to develop good skills of self-management, the deck may be stacked against us. The habit of giving in to particular impulses can be all but unbreakable.

In addition to the control of desires, self-management also involves the control of impulses deriving from emotion. While it is a mistake to think of emotions as nonrational feelings, an emotion may generate feelings which make it difficult to act to achieve our objectives. Think, for example, of losing your temper in a meeting with the boss, or of vengeful feelings toward an ex-spouse with whom you share the custody of children, or fearfulness in the presence of an intimidating person whom you need to impress, or feelings of discouragement in the middle of a long and demanding project. When our emotions are in harmony with our reflective judgments of how to act, they can be powerful allies, but when harmony is lacking, our emotions may oppose us at every step.

As with desires, the capacity for managing our emotions depends on the habits we have developed. Consistently losing your temper or avoiding any risky undertakings because of anxiety are good ways to ensure that when you want to control your anger or anxiety, you will be fighting an uphill battle. Conversely, we develop the ability to exercise control over desires or emotions by actually exercising control. Usually we try to teach children these skills by having them do on a small scale what they will later need to do on a larger scale. Learning not to eat all the Halloween candy at once or not to throw a tantrum when your parent does not stop at the toy store may be major accomplishments for a child. They are also preparation for the sort of disciplines needed for effective adult living.

However, this sort of training, even if effective in childhood, must be sustained by continual practice. We may learn what it means to defer immediate gratification and limit our self-indulgence in childhood, but it is only by the continual exercise of our powers of resistance that these powers develop into habits. Acquiring habits of self-control calls for sustained effort, but it also makes some things easier in the long-run. Although even the most disciplined person can experience difficult struggles, habits of self-control allow us to override some impulses with minimal effort. The beginning jogger who has started an exercise program may fight every time with the temptation to skip exercise today, but the person who has continued the practice is often able to ignore such impulses without a struggle.

We have names for some of the powers to control particular impulses. The old-fashioned name for the trait which results in control of desires is temperance. Possessing this trait does not mean that you lack desires or that you never try to satisfy your desires. It is instead a matter of being able to satisfy your desires in ways you judge to be good. The ability to control your fear or anxiety is called courage. We need courage any time what we judge to be worth doing involves personal risk—whether the risk is to physical security, reputation, career, finances, or something else we value. Courage does not mean taking unwise risks, nor does it mean the absence of fear. It is the trait by means of which we can feel fear, but not let it keep us from doing what we judge to be important or worthwhile.

Aristotle concluded that human excellences or virtues such as courage or temperance are acquired through practice.[6] He compares the way we learn these traits to the way we learn the skill involved in some craft, such as woodworking. Instruction is involved, but it is by engaging in the activity, approximating the skill, getting correction, and finally discovering how it feels to get it right that we internalize the habits necessary for continually using the skill. When you are trying to learn the game of tennis, it may take you many attempts before you come close to the stroke your instructor is seeking to produce. When you get it right and recognize that you have done so, you need to practice until you can do it habitually. From a platform of desirable habits, you are ready to move to the next level and improve your game.

Similarly, it is by practicing control over our impulses that we develop our powers to exercise control when we need to. Repeatedly giving in to impulses that conflict with good judgment turns us into people with a diminished capacity for overruling our impulses. By following such policies, we may remain virtual beginners all our lives in the art of dealing with desires and emotions that can usurp the authority of judgment. Moreover, unless we continue to use the skills of self-management we do develop, they may atrophy through lack of practice. But by diligently cultivating our skills, we can prepare ourselves for asserting control over our lives when it is most important to do so.

COGNITIVE HABITS AND STRATEGIES

Since self-management involves bringing our impulses under the control of our judgment, it calls for the cultivation of habits of reflection. Many of our acts are done in unreflective ways. Ordinarily we get dressed, drive to work, exchange greetings, and hundreds of other activities without thinking much about what we are doing. The ability to act unreflectively is generally a good thing. If we always had to consciously attend to what we are doing, we could not develop complex skills which involve learning to do some things without thinking. However, our lack of reflection is not just a matter of going on automatic pilot much of the time. Whether or not our minds are engaged in the activity, we may act without considering why we are doing an act, whether it is worth doing, whether there are alternatives that might achieve our purposes better, and whether our purposes are producing the kind of life we want.

Not all action requires or is worth much reflection, and anyone who tried to be reflective about everything would be a long way down the road to lunacy. However, it is possible to become so habitual and unreflective that you are hardly exercising rational control at all. A person may go to school, get married, have children, and perform a job without ever considering how these pursuits fit in with her primary values and concerns. Doing what you have been conditioned to do or simply doing what others are doing or doing what seems easy can be an abdication of the human capacity to choose and take responsibility for your life.

Self-management involves conscious choices to stand back occasionally and make reflective judgments about what you are doing, what you want to achieve, and how particular impulses can be integrated with the kind of life you are seeking. The results of this reflection should include judgments about desires and the formation of what some philosophers call second-order desires.[7] A second-order desire is a desire about what desires to have. For example, suppose I have a sedentary lifestyle and begin to give serious thought to developing some kind of exercise program. I become convinced that this will enable me to control my weight, become healthier, deal with stress, etcetera. On the basis of this thinking, I decide to exercise. However, I still have no desire to exercise. In fact, I desire not to expend the energy and effort involved. My reflective efforts, however, have resulted in a desire to alter my slothful impulses. I have formed a second-order desire to get rid of my desire not to exercise and possibly even to acquire a desire to exercise. The kind of control we call freedom of the will involves the power to form such second-order desires and to shape my first-order desires into conformity with them.

In addition to becoming reflective about my way of life, I may also apply conscious strategies for controlling impulses that conflict with reflective judgments. One strategy is to imagine the long-term consequences of giving in to an impulse. What are the likely results if I continue to give in? Will I be pleased with carrying twenty extra pounds, or with not completing my degree on time, or with not being able to play the piano? How will I feel about myself? Will I feel shame at my lack of control? Will I be proud of the kind of life I am living? Would I want my children to live in this way? Part of the power of impulses comes from the way they focus our attention on the short-term and block our awareness of the larger context of a decision. By consciously considering the impulse in a larger perspective, we can often rob it of some of its power.

Another cognitive strategy is to confront directly messages you are giving yourself which contribute to the power of impulses you want to resist. For example, you might have allowed yourself to think that you can't control a particular impulse, either because your inability is just like everyone else's or because you have a special problem produced by a difficult past. Or you might have told yourself that you are only giving in this one time—that later you will start to act in a disciplined way. Or you might have thought to yourself that discipline is overrated—that it takes away from the spontaneous enjoyment of life and makes you overly rigid.[8] Rationalizing and making excuses and even deceiving ourselves create obstacles to self-control which need to be dismantled by thinking directly about how half-baked some of our self-communications are. The sense of powerlessness produced by these messages may disintegrate when we confront them directly with our critical minds.

A related cognitive strategy is to recognize and avoid activities that are feeding an uncontrolled impulse. Suppose the control of anger is a problem. Anger is a product of certain ways of thinking about another person's actions. You think, for example, that Sam has hurt you unjustly. If you were to discover that Sam was not the one who hurt you or that Sam had a good reason for what he did, or that the hurt was unintentional, you would not be able to feel anger towards Sam. You might still feel frustrated, but emotions like anger depend on thought patterns consistent with the emotion's cognitive structure. It is possible to feed an emotion by dwelling on particular thoughts. Sometimes you can work yourself into a state of anger by reminding yourself of the despicable nature of a wrong done to you. Similarly, it is possible to refuse to feed an emotion by not dwelling on certain thoughts or by enlarging your thinking to consider the possibility of alternative viewpoints, or by thinking about whether this incident is worth all the energy.

Still another strategy is to determine some little thing you can do to resist the impulse rather than trying to conquer the whole thing completely. A husband and father, recognizing that his extramarital affair could tear his family apart, felt powerless to break it off. His minister suggested that he focus all his energy on not ringing the doorbell to the woman's apartment. As odd as it seems, concentrating his efforts on this choice enabled him to end the affair. Similarly, deciding that you are not going to drink for this one evening may be manageable, while trying to decide for the rest of your life may be overwhelming. Hence, Alcoholics Anonymous suggests its members attempt sobriety for "one day at a time."

There are other strategies, but no matter how easy it may seem on paper, resisting real-life impulses can be inescapably difficult. Human beings are capable of the most complex forms of shortsightedness, rationalization, and self-deception. Gaining self-control is a continual battle which is never completely won. It can, however, be lost by policies of indulgence that lead to diminished powers to exercise rational control over our lives.

THE EASY WAY

The path which seems easiest may not get you where you want to go. Developing self-control is far from easy; it is difficult and demanding. But facing up to difficult and challenging tasks, rather than assuming you can do things the easy way, is often the only means of building the life you want. A student who was having difficulty finishing his graduate thesis recognized that his problem was an inability to give up pleasant distractions and get to work. He had never had to work very hard in school before and was stuck in a childish mode of avoiding what he knew he needed to do. His lack of good work habits made the thesis a more monumental undertaking than it would otherwise have been. He wanted to finish the degree, but he did not want to give up the pleasant diversions which kept him from doing what he needed. As a result he spent endless hours lamenting how difficult it was and in the end gave up his goal.

Another man habitually took what seemed the easiest paths in his personal relationships. He went to a counselor, complaining that a girlfriend was clinging to him. He wanted to keep her on the string, but he didn't want her around all the time. The counselor suggested that he tell the woman directly what he wanted. The man was reluctant to do so. He didn't want to lose the girl completely. He just wanted the freedom to see her only when he wanted. He decided to try to get the counselor to tell the woman (Sally) that he had diagnosed her boyfriend's problem and that she should limit her visits for mental health reasons. The counselor replied:

> If I did what you wanted me to do, I would deprive you of the glorious opportunity to buckle down, for perhaps the first time in your life, to solve this difficult situation and gain some confidence that you actually *can* face and solve tough situations that you encounter. I would also thus connive to help Sally avoid making her own difficult decisions about whether to accept you on your terms or go on behaving as a big baby, as she does now. So my answer: a flat no. I intend to do you the service of forcing you, if possible, to face life this time, so that you may learn how to cope with it and with yourself for a change and how to modify some of your obviously self-defeating short-range hedonism.[9]

Sometimes people buy into the illusion that acting in their self-interest means taking shortcuts that avoid the pain or stress of doing something difficult. But this pattern of living typically leads to more difficulties and strenuous efforts of avoidance in the future. By learning to accept responsibility and face up to difficult but necessary tasks directly, we acquire the means to more effectively achieve our interest. By doing what is hard in the short-run, we often discover a path that ultimately is easier.

BECOMING SELF-DISCIPLINED

The primary thesis of this book is that a serious concern with self-interest involves us in considerations about what kind of self to become. It is evident that when self-interest is understood to involve any goals beyond immediate gratification, its pursuit calls for becoming the kind of person who is able to defer gratification. It also calls for developing and preserving the capacity to use reflective judgment to coordinate conflicting impulses. Hence, high on the list of considerations in determining our interest is discovering how to acquire and maintain the character traits needed for effective self-management.

What we do helps to determine whether we actually develop the character traits we will need, but it is difficult to take seriously the effects of individual actions on our character. We are inclined to discount those effects, regarding our skills of self-management as relatively fixed. We can see how our actions are related to short-term and even to some long-term goals. However, in any particular case it is tempting to tell ourselves that a little more indulgence does not matter. Unfortunately, the cumulative result of our failures to exercise self-control is a decline in the capacity to exercise it, and we are not usually in a position to determine at what point our capacity will severely limit our pursuits. We may think that we can exercise reflective control when we want to, but allow unreflective impulses to take over occasionally. The problem is that the part of our lives where we give up the pursuit of our own best interest may expand more than we can predict. Trying to maintain the capacity for control while at the same time failing to exercise control is a little like trying to keep a tiger as a pet; it's a risky venture.

When we fail to become self-disciplined or fail to preserve our powers of self-management, we are failing to act in our self-interest. We usually think of the character traits needed for self-management as related to giving others their due, and it is certainly true that exhibiting respect for others calls for traits such as courage and temperance and patience. But even if we don't see the need to develop such traits for others, we can at least recognize that failing to develop these traits will block our own attempts to fashion a desirable life. Achieving the life we want means becoming the right kind of self: a self that is able to act on the basis of reflective judgment instead of being controlled by unreflective impulses that conflict with good judgment. Our judgments of self-interest will always be distorted unless we can sufficiently take into account how our actions are contributing to or tearing down our efforts to build such a self.

Chapter Two

THE RANGE OF HUMAN CONCERNS

If there be any real good-will or kindness at all, it must be disinterested; for the most useful action imaginable loses all appearance of benevolence, as soon as we discern that it only flowed from self-love, or interest. (Francis Hutcheson[1])

Take, for example, the doctrine that man only acts selfishly—that is, from the consideration that acting in one way will afford him more pleasure than acting in another. This rests on no fact in the world, but it has had a wide acceptance as being the only reasonable theory. (Charles Peirce[2])

Ideas can be enticing. Sometimes we find ourselves attracted by an idea, not so much on the basis of evidence, but because it provides a way of thinking that seems congenial. When we think in accordance with the idea, it is as if we gain an insight that clarifies and simplifies matters. We can scarcely even imagine how things could be otherwise. Even if someone gives us a proof that the idea is mistaken, we find ourselves slipping back into the comfortable patterns of thought it provides, believing that the idea must be true nevertheless.

One of those enticing ideas that exerts a powerful influence on many people is the view that self-interested motivations underlie all human actions. This idea offers a way of interpreting human behavior that radically simplifies our understanding of why people do what they do. According to this view, alternative motivations for behavior, such as concern for the good of others, do not exist. When we appear to display such concern, what we really exhibit is a disguised form of self-interest, for we only seek the good of others as a means to achieving our own good. From the mind of the college sophomore, who believes he has found an important truth about human nature, to the works of scholars in the social sciences, the idea of universal egoism is accepted as an obvious truth.[3] Whether this "truth" is supported by the evidence is often a matter of indifference to those who are convinced by it. They find it difficult even to imagine the possibility of being wrong.

For many people the idea of universal egoism is connected with experiences of disillusionment. Few of us can hear reports that a politician or a businessperson has done something apparently good or praiseworthy without wondering what personal benefit he or she expected to get from the action. Our suspicions of self-serving motives have been verified often enough that we respond to accounts of apparently noble or heroic actions with an almost reflexive cynicism. We have learned that people can put up a good front, strategically hiding their self-serving motives, and we find ourselves doubting that all is what it appears to be. Journalists know that a healthy suspicion enables them to keep looking until they uncover truths that someone would like to conceal. Those of us who read their accounts of corruption and duplicity can easily form the habit of expecting the worst of people, and often enough our expectations are confirmed.

It is tempting to generalize our suspicions into an all-encompassing account of human motivation. If actions that appear to be motivated by a concern for the welfare of others or some noble ideal often turn out to be forms of self-seeking, then perhaps looking hard enough would reveal all actions to be motivated by self-interested concerns. Such a sweeping hypothesis appears to provide a simple method of explaining a wide range of behavior. It gives us a way of interpreting what other people do, as well as a way of construing our own actions.

Sometimes this idea is proclaimed as a liberating concept. Viewing pressures to behave unselfishly as oppressive ploys by which others seek to control our behavior, self-help writer, Harry Browne, urges us to recognize that both we and anyone urging unselfishness are motivated by selfishness. It is just that we find gratification in different ways:

> One man devotes his life to helping the poor. Another one lies and steals. Still another person tries to create better products and services for which he hopes to be paid handsomely. One woman devotes herself to her husband and children. Another seeks a career as a singer.[4]

All of these diverse activities, says Browne, have exactly the same motivation. Whether one lives as a thief or as a humanitarian, the motive will always be to act in "ways he believes will make him feel good or will remove discomfort from his life."[5] The means may be different, but the end is always a person's pursuit of his or her own happiness. So, Browne tells us, "...we can't avoid a very significant conclusion: *Everyone is selfish* ...everyone selfishly seeks his own happiness."[6] Once we recognize this, Browne thinks we can be freed to pursue our own selfish ends without any troubling need to restrict our behavior. We can with a clear conscience do whatever we think will enable us to "feel good" and "avoid discomfort."

One striking thing about this view is the certainty with which it is advanced. We might have expected a thesis about *all* human actions to be supported by mountains of empirical evidence. But this author and others who advance the thesis of universal egoism feel little need to produce any evidence at all. Simply announcing the idea is thought to be sufficient. If we understand the motivation attributed to everyone, we should simply see that it applies to any action whatsoever. Rather than reasons for thinking that this thesis is true, what we typically get is a challenge to prove it false, as if the failure to do so would amount to proving it true.

One obvious way to respond to such a challenge is by posing apparent counterexamples to the idea of universal egoism. What about the missionary who gives away her food to aid the hungry and dies as a result? What about the truck driver who stops to help a stranger with car trouble? What about a businesswoman who gives an accurate report of her income, even when she can fudge some, with only a minuscule chance of being caught?

The response to each of these examples follows the same strategy: either finding a possible motivation that could be labeled self-interested and claiming that it is the *real* motivation or suggesting that the action in question is not genuinely voluntary and that the thesis applies only to voluntary actions: The missionary may have starved herself, but that is because she was seeking a heavenly reward. The truck driver stopped, but this is because helping others makes him feel good. The businesswoman reported her income accurately, but this is because she had a pathological fear of getting caught, stemming from some unfortunate experience in childhood.

No matter how far-fetched or implausible, the egoistic interpretation is typically advanced with a decisiveness and confidence that even if the particular selfish motive suggested is mistaken, something like it is bound to be true. Of course, no one with any experience of the world doubts that many actions that appear to be unselfish have hidden motivations. But for some it is almost an article of faith to be defended with dogmatic assurance that all behavior, no matter how much appearances suggest otherwise, is rooted in a concern for some personal benefit. If that motivation is not obvious, it will be claimed, it *must*, nevertheless, be there.

SOME CLARIFICATIONS

One confusion that often arises in discussions of this type is between selfishness and self-interest. Claiming that an act is selfish means something different from claiming that it is motivated by self-interest. For example, if I shop for groceries so that I will have something to cook for dinner, I have acted in my self-interest, but it seems odd to call this action selfish. Labeling an act as selfish typically suggests that one has acted in a way that disregards the interests of others who should have been considered. If I spend the family budget on stereo equipment for myself and thereby deprive my children of the shoes they need, I have behaved selfishly. Showing that I acted to achieve a personal benefit may reveal my act to be self-interested, but it is insufficient to show it to be selfish.[7]

Probably the most charitable interpretation of the idea of universal egoism is to understand it to mean that all voluntary acts are motivated by self-interest. However, if we take into account self-destructive behavior of the kind described in the last chapter, it is clearly untrue to say that people are motivated to do what is actually in their self-interest. Nor can we say that people always act to bring about what they believe to be their self-interest. There are too many examples of knowing that something is bad for you, yet doing it anyway. So is there another way to understand this claim which might make it at least arguable?

One possibility is to construe universal egoism as a thesis about the kinds of desires capable of motivating behavior.[8] Suppose that we call a desire whose object is some benefit for the self a self-interested desire. Potential objects of such desires include such things as wealth, power, security, health, pleasure, status, love, etcetera. The thesis of universal egoism could be interpreted to mean that the only desires capable of motivating us are self-interested desires.

This way of characterizing the thesis depends on a use of the word "benefit" to refer to things which are generally regarded as valuable to people. However, whether or not a particular object is beneficial, all things considered, depends on both the context in which the object is sought and the nature of the particular self. So fulfilling a self-interested desire, as it is defined here, need not be in one's self-interest and may very well be opposed to one's self-interest. The self-interested objects are benefits only in the sense of being generally desired.

In claiming that the only motivating desires are self-interested, the advocate of universal egoism is not denying that we may have other types of desires. For example, we could have desires to benefit others (benevolent desires), desires to harm others (malevolent desires) or desires to behave morally (moral desires). What is claimed is that these desires are all dependent on self-interested desires. We desire these other things only as means of satisfying desires directed towards benefits for the self.

For example, suppose that a mother desires her children to flourish. The egoist will claim that the achievement of this end is a means to some self-interested end such as the vicarious satisfaction a parent might get from her children's achievements. Or suppose that one has a desire to keep her promise in some case where it is difficult to do so. The egoist might claim that this moral desire is a means to a self-interested end such as gaining a good reputation in the community. In any particular case universal egoism posits a self-interested desire as the ultimate motivator of behavior.

The first thing to notice about this thesis is how extraordinary it is. What is proposed is a catch-all explanation for anything anyone does. No one ever acts out of concern for another person—it's always some desire for personal benefit. No one ever acts out of concern for a moral ideal—acting morally is just another disguised form of self-seeking. No one ever acts out of malicious desires toward others—all malicious acts are motivated by something one hopes to get for the self. It would be remarkable if these claims were true.

AN EXPANDING MODEL

People who advance this thesis are often absolutely convinced of the truth of their view. This confidence is in many cases accompanied by a contempt for anyone who stubbornly resists recognizing their account as correct. The advocates see themselves as worldly wise compared to anyone naive enough to believe in such things as benevolent actions. Why are they so convinced? The primary reason is that one who starts to conceive things according to the model this view expounds, finds the model expanding in such a way as to exclude other ways of conceiving things. The model is like a point of view on human behavior that squeezes out any alternative points of view.

For example, a counselor, who was dealing with a woman who had endured years in an abusive relationship, was asked why the woman had stayed so long. Without hesitation, the counselor replied, "She must have been getting something from the relationship." Unquestionably, we can often gain insight into what people do by asking, "What did he or she get from the action?" But the counselor was not merely adopting a helpful point of view; she was asserting dogmatically that people always have some self-interested motive beneath the surface.

Why should we think so? In the case of the woman who is behaving in self-destructive ways, is it more plausible to say that she is benefitting in some way from her actions or that she is in the grip of some self-destructive impulses or enduring the abuse because of a misguided allegiance to a faulty moral ideal? There are any number of ways of explaining this behavior that make no reference to benefit of any kind. What, other than a dogmatic conviction that we can construe all behavior according to the simple model of self-interest, would lead us to think that positing a self-interested desire underlying self-destructive behavior is at all convincing? From the point of view of helping the woman make better decisions in the future, would it be better for her to think, "I was gaining something after all," or to think, "I wasn't sufficiently attentive to my own best interest"? We can undoubtedly think about this situation in terms of gains and losses, but this is unlikely to get us much insight into the real motivation of the action. For that we need a much more complex model of human behavior.

The idea that the only motivating desires we have are self-interested can only survive if we pay little attention to the variety of desires people actually have. While a person can certainly have desires for things we classify as benefits, isn't it possible to desire something while realizing that it is not a benefit? Imagine a relationship with someone who has repeatedly abused your trust and taken advantage of you. You might be fully aware that a relationship with this person is not good for you, yet desire it anyway. Claiming that you are motivated by a desire for a good because relationships in general are good or because there are good elements in this terrible relationship is suggesting a possible hypothesis about the real motivation, but in cases of this sort there is often little reason to think that the proposed hypothetical desire is actually what motivates a person. Observation of ourselves and others strongly suggests that sometimes we are moved by desires that are fundamentally self-destructive. It may be said that acting in accordance with such desires is irrational, but that is no reason for denying that we do so.

In addition to possessing self-destructive desires, people also possess desires to harm others. Sometimes we want someone who has done us wrong to suffer for it. Sometimes we desire to get revenge against someone. Are these desires for personal benefit? It might be claimed that what we are really desiring in such cases are feelings of satisfaction that we expect from the other person's suffering or from "getting even." But in many cases there is no expectation of any such feelings. You can desire the other person to suffer without expecting to get anything from it. You can desire revenge, even with the realization that it will give you no satisfaction and you will suffer greatly in the attempt. Again, there may be something irrational about acting on the basis of such desires, but the evidence suggests that actual human behavior is not always rational.

When we ask the question of what desires people are motivated by, we are not asking what desires they would be well advised to be motivated by. What desires actually motivate behavior is an issue to be dealt with by judging what account best fits with what people do and what they report. If we find that a particular model of motivation is inadequate to deal with the complexity of actual behavior, we may need to look for a more comprehensive model.

BENEVOLENT DESIRES

Cases of self-destructive behavior or malevolent behavior are troublesome for the theory of universal egoism because they suggest that the model proposed in that theory is overly simple. However, they are not the kinds of cases people who defend universal egoism have in mind or pay any attention to when they assert their view. Their central focus is on the denial of motivation by benevolent desires. According to their view, any act to promote the good of another is motivated by a desire for one's own benefit, not by a desire for another's good.

Maintaining this thesis typically depends on the use of several strategies for explaining away apparently benevolent actions. In cases of acting for the good of others where it is difficult to conceive any benefit gained by the action, say because death is an immediate result, defenders of universal egoism sometimes resort to expected benefits in an afterlife. The missionary who starved to death because she was giving away her food to others may appear to be motivated by benevolent desires, but the *real* motivation was her hope of a heavenly reward. If someone seriously suggests this interpretation, we need to clarify what it means. Does it mean that the missionary thinks to herself, "If I give away my food and die, God will reward me"? Or is the claim that although she does not think about giving away her food in order to get the heavenly reward, this motivation somehow unconsciously underlies her benevolent deeds?

Claims about unconscious motivations are notoriously difficult to verify. The thesis of universal egoism is going to be on shaky grounds if it must resort to claims about what we desire unconsciously, and it appears that the only reason for doing so in this kind of case is a desperate attempt to save the thesis, not any real evidence. On the other hand, if it is claimed that the missionary was consciously doing benevolent deeds in order to get a heavenly reward, this would suggest a kind of spiritual immaturity that her religious community would probably judge to be defective. The mature believer is expected to get beyond the point of acting only for reward, just as a morally mature person is expected to get beyond acting only from fear of punishment. However, if the missionary has come to the point where she desires to benefit others without any consideration of reward for herself, her desire is not functioning as a means to a self-interested end. Even if her benevolent desires were initially rooted in a desire for reward, they may have become independent of their causal origin. A boy who starts to play the piano because his father promises an increase in his allowance for each hour spent in practice, might very well develop a desire for piano playing which remains long after the increases cease. If that occurs, it would be a confusion to say that he has no real desire motivating him to play the piano, only a desire for a nonexistent reward. The original cause of the desire is simply irrelevant to deciding what motivates him now.

If anyone remains convinced that appeals to the afterlife can furnish a defense for universal egoism, we have only to imagine the same kind of deed done by someone who has no belief in God, karma or continued existence. If the unbeliever performs a sacrificial act, which will predictably lead to death, are we to say that it must flow from a self-interested desire? While we can imagine cases where someone might be very concerned with doing what would enhance his reputation after death, there can also be cases where there is no such motivating concern.

Suppose we confine ourselves to less dramatic cases than sacrificial deaths to benefit others. What strategies are available to the defender of universal egoism in more ordinary situations? In many cases of apparent benevolence, we can point to benefits that an individual might reasonably expect to receive from helping others. In communal situations where you can expect to deal with another person on a regular basis or where the person has the power to enhance or harm your reputation, there are often self-interested reasons for doing what will produce good will and a positive testimony from others. So we can imagine that apparently benevolent behavior in a context where others have the power to help or hurt us could conceivably arise out of reflection on the long-term benefits of benevolent actions. As long as the cost of benefitting others is not too great, it could, in many cases, be regarded as an investment in the future.

Even if this were the case, however, it would not remove the possibility of being motivated by benevolent desires. Of course, if you had to think on each occasion, "I am benefitting Fred in the expectation that this will result in more long-term benefits for me," your desire to benefit Fred would not be a benevolent motivation. But what if reflection on the likely paybacks of benevolent behavior gave rise to a policy of acting for the good of others and later this way of acting became more or less habitual? Conceivably you might acquire some genuinely benevolent desires which are independent of their origin. Just as one can acquire a taste for gardening by engaging in the activity and learning to like it, it is possible to learn to enjoy doing what benefits others.

In reality it is unlikely that all the displays of benevolence we find are the result of rational calculation. Psychological research shows that children often respond spontaneously to other children with the apparent intention of aiding the other child or alleviating the other child's pain.[9] Seeing another in need causes us distress, leaving us with inclinations to help, though these inclinations may be suppressed by environmental influences hostile to helping behavior. The assumption that humans don't have or can't develop any benevolent motivating desires seems plausible only if we disregard considerable evidence to the contrary. Actual behavior gives us reason to think that sympathetic and benevolent desires sometimes motivate our actions, though in many situations they are decidedly weaker than conflicting self-interested desires, and they are unlikely to be as strong when we move from the circle of family and friends to acquaintances and strangers.

PSYCHIC BENEFITS

It might argued that in any case where a benevolent desire exists, it can only function as a motivator if the desire is connected with psychic rewards or punishments. The individual who has come to acquire a taste for helping behavior has learned to associate this kind of behavior with good feelings. The child who is distressed at the pain of a playmate acts to alleviate the distress. The person who has been trained to feel guilty about not helping others attempts to avoid feelings of guilt. So even if we have a case where it is unrealistic to expect a tangible payback, such as the truck driver who helps a stranger he will be unlikely to see again, we can look for a psychic payback, and this psychic benefit is the *real* motivation of the action. The truck driver performs his good deed in order to feel good, or to avoid feeling bad.

This sort of argument involves a number of questionable assumptions. One is the assumption that when an action produces a psychic benefit, that benefit can be identified as the motivation of the action. Suppose that my yard needs mowing, and I reluctantly drag out the lawn mower to begin the job. After I get into the work, I begin to feel a sense of satisfaction about being outdoors on a nice day and maybe about getting the job done. Can we conclude that I decided to mow the yard in order to get the satisfaction? Surely not. I may not have anticipated it at all, and even if I did, I may have had a variety of concerns other than achieving the satisfaction. Perhaps I wanted to avoid another unpleasant task, and the yard was a handy excuse for doing so. The point is that finding some psychic benefit (or potential psychic benefit) does not by itself assure us that we have discovered why an action was done. At best it only gives us a possible motive.

Furthermore, in some cases it does not even give us a possible motive, for in some cases a psychic benefit can only occur if a person is aiming at something other than the benefit. Suppose I have heard that people who read and discuss literary works gain some kind of pleasure or satisfaction from doing so. Hearing this, I decide that I want to get some of this satisfaction for myself. So I read a book and attend a group where this book is being discussed. Imagine that I don't care at all about the book or about literature. I just want the pleasure it might give me. It is a safe bet that I am not going to find what I am after, for this sort of satisfaction is only available to someone whose attention and admiration is engaged by the literature. To get this satisfaction, I have to learn to value and appreciate literature for its own sake, not just for the satisfaction it might produce. Aiming directly at the satisfaction is almost a guaranteed way of missing it.

In many cases, positive states of mind are best viewed as by-products of engaging in an activity you find worthwhile. When you achieve something you regard as worthwhile, the natural result is a sense of satisfaction. But receiving this psychic by-product depends on having motivating concerns to engage in the worthwhile activity which are independent of the concern for satisfaction. Let us return to the case of the truck driver. How is it that the truck driver allegedly gets good feelings from helping others? One possibility is that the truck driver has come to think of helping others as an important and worthwhile activity and feels the satisfaction usually connected with doing something worthwhile. But in that case the motivating desire is the desire to help others, and the satisfaction is a result of fulfilling that desire.

It can be tempting in this kind of argument to look for an example of benevolent behavior in which a person gets no psychic reward, but it would be very odd to claim that in order to have a motivating desire to help others, one must not get any pleasure or satisfaction from helping them. In fact, getting pleasure or satisfaction is exactly what we expect of a person who is genuinely benevolent. Someone who helped others, but felt no satisfaction, or who had negative feelings and hated every minute of giving aid, might be commended for endurance, but would not be a model of benevolence. Aristotle argues that part of acquiring a virtuous character trait is learning to experience pleasure at acting in accordance with the character trait.[10] To be courageous is to feel some pleasure or satisfaction at controlling your fears. To be compassionate is to get some pleasure or satisfaction at responding to the suffering of others. The absence of proper feelings can indicate that one has not fully internalized the concerns that go with a character trait.

If benevolent desires produce psychic benefits, this is not because they are self-interested; it is because someone who cares about others can regard helping them as a valuable accomplishment, and we tend to receive positive feelings from doing things we value. Those positive feelings furnish some evidence of having concerns for things other than our own benefit. A person who is motivated only by self-interested desires and has no real concern for others, should either get no satisfaction from helping them, or should regard any satisfaction as an unfortunate product of irrational conditioning that may need to be eliminated.

DEFINITIONAL TRUTHS

I have noted already that universal egoism tends to be held with a steadfast certainty. When confronted by empirical evidence of benevolent behavior, the defender of this thesis is sure that the apparent benevolence can be explained away. If all else fails, there is a strategy used by advocates of universal egoism to make their case airtight against any counterexamples. It involves claiming that a person must be motivated by self-interested desires because what moves her to act is always *her own* desires. Whether we desire to help others or to steal from them, we are doing what we desire to do.

This defense rests on a major confusion. Even if we suppose that the basis of action is always some desire, showing that the motivating desire belonged to the person doing the action does not show that desire to be self-interested. Whether or not a desire is self-interested depends on its object. If the object of my desire is a benefit for myself, I can classify it as a self-interested desire. But if what moves me to action is a desire for someone else's benefit, my desire is not self-interested.

Suppose the egoist gives the following reply: I can define my terms any way I like, and what *I* mean by a self-interested desire is simply any desire of the person who performs an action. In that case, the egoist has given us a way to claim that egoism is true, but the cost of defending the thesis in this way is to render it trivial. Claiming that people act on the basis of their own desires or concerns is not the striking thesis that we thought the egoist was making. We could admit that claim and yet still assert that sometimes people act out of concern for the welfare of others. Indeed, we might even claim that sometimes people build their whole lives on promoting communal ends which require considerable sacrifice of personal benefits. The egoist is not denying any of this. By retreating to an idiosyncratic definition of "self-interested desires," the egoist may be claiming something true, but has ceased to say anything important.

When the discussion began, we believed we were discussing a striking thesis about human nature and human motivation. For such a thesis empirical evidence would be of great importance. In the course of the discussion, however, it becomes clear that the egoist is not willing to entertain any evidence as a possible counterexample. This might seem to be a strength of the theory, but it is actually a weakness. If the terms of the thesis are defined in such a way that any *possible* action is consistent with it, it looks more like a proposal to use words in a particular way, rather than a claim about any empirical facts.

The distinction between self-interested actions and those that are not self-interested ordinarily allows us to mark off actions motivated by the pursuit of money or power or sex or some other personal benefit from actions motivated by a concern for the well-being of others or for fulfilling some moral ideal. If this distinction is erased by some definitional maneuver, nothing will have changed factually, but we may have more difficulty pointing to a difference that we sometimes judge to be important. The egoist wants to suggest that all these behaviors are alike in some sense, but focusing on the sense in which they are all alike can conceal differences that it might be crucial to notice.

This problem can be seen in the discussion of the self-help writer quoted earlier. He tells us that the person devoted to aiding humanity and the person who lies and steals have exactly the same motive. From this, he suggests that there is a kind of equivalency for each kind of life. But even if there is a sense of "selfishly motivated" in which all of these different types of lives can be judged alike, imagining that the choice between them is arbitrary or that there might not be good reasons for preferring one sort of life to another is outrageous. Though we may define our terms as we like, we should not be surprised if bizarre definitions lead us into errors of thought and action.

CHOOSING A LIFE

Even if we thought that all actions were motivated by self-interested desires, we could still give consideration to the question of which self-interested desires we want to be motivated by, but the chances are that this way of thinking would close off any serious consideration of some types of life. This limitation is particularly likely if we buy into the idea that our only motivation is ultimately to "feel good" and "avoid discomfort." Many of the things people are concerned about draw their attention away from the goal of feeling good, involving considerable risk of negative feelings. Is having and raising a child to be recommended on the grounds that it is likely to involve more pleasure than pain? Undoubtedly, there are satisfactions in childrearing, but if we compare these satisfactions to the personal sacrifices involved, surely there are more efficient ways to get good feelings.

Many of the things we choose are chosen because we judge certain activities and ways of living to be worthier or more admirable than others, and it is artificial to try to reduce our judgments of worth to judgments about personal benefits.[11] People often think that benefitting their children or benefitting the community or developing their artistic talents or understanding how the laws of nature work are worthy ends to pursue. They build into their lives a variety of concerns for things which could easily be liabilities for a person who was concerned only with maximizing personal benefits.

The potential range of human concerns is great. There are people who devote themselves to looking for a cure for cancer or raising a family or providing a needed service or protecting the defenseless. Seeing all of these varied activities as forms of self-seeking obscures as much as it reveals. In particular, it obscures our awareness of some pursuits as more valuable than others and of the potential for building a self capable of caring about and pursuing valuable ends.

For the person who has developed a wide range of concerns, the question of whether a particular act is self-interested is often unimportant. People who risked their own lives to rescue Jews from Nazi atrocities during World War II were found by researchers to have built into their own identities a strong sense of a common humanity by means of which they identified with the Jews.[12] Their actions could be characterized as acting out of benevolent desires, but given the particular identity they had developed, they were also acting out of their own interest in maintaining a valued identity.

For a less expansive self, however, the question of whether to cultivate desires other than self-interested ones may be of crucial importance. For such persons, limiting the possible options prematurely means losing the opportunity of considering potentially worthwhile ways of living. Only if we can imagine caring about things other than the self, can we expand our thinking to include the full range of possibilities. Once we recognize that it is possible to be motivated by concerns other than self-interested ones, we are in a position to think seriously about what motivations to build into the self we aspire to become.

Chapter Three

GETTING WHAT YOU WANT

In this world there are only two tragedies. One is not getting what one wants, and the other is getting it. (Oscar Wilde[1])

I was in a dull state of nerves, such as everybody is occasionally liable to; unsusceptible to enjoyment or pleasurable excitement.... In this frame of mind it occurred to me to put the question directly to myself: "Suppose that all your objects in life were realized...would this be a great joy and happiness to you?" And an irrepressible self-consciousness distinctly answered, "No!" (John Stuart Mill[2])

Getting what you want is not the same as wanting what you get. In fact, one of the most fearful forms of poetic justice is to invest your whole being in an attempt to secure some object of perceived value, only to discover that what you have gained is worth very little. Our legends portray this truth vividly: Think, for example, of the story of King Midas who received his wish for gold, but destroyed his life in the process. Sometimes the worst punishment is to get exactly what you are striving for and to find it empty and unsatisfying.

Recognizing this danger does not require us to avoid trying to get what we want. It would be bizarre for someone to follow a policy of refusing to satisfy any wants—only seeking something if it is unwanted. However, there is something equally defective about a policy of uncritically assuming that satisfying any want makes us better off. What is needed is some way of distinguishing between wants with a strong claim to satisfaction and wants that need to be ignored or altered.

All of us have had the experience of wanting something that we suspect is not good for us. We might want another piece of cake or a cigarette or a sexual encounter and be aware that the want goes against our better judgment. In most cases of this kind the particular want conflicts with something else we want, something that we would reflectively judge to be more important. I might want to vegetate in front of the TV set each evening and yet find that this prevents me from getting the benefits of the exercise program I have planned. I might want to avoid the hard work of writing for several hours each day, but realize that without setting aside a regular time, I am unlikely to achieve my goal of writing a best-selling novel. Conflicting wants call for choice, and usually the refusal to choose amounts to a choice.

But how is it possible to prioritize my wants? I could say that the priority is established by deciding what I want most, but that would be unhelpful, since the idea of wanting something most is unclear. Does it mean that I have a very strong subjective experience of desiring? In that case it does not have a particularly strong claim to satisfaction, for some of the things I want most in that sense could be precisely the things I despise myself for wanting. I could want very much to ignore the questionable activities of my company, not rocking the boat, yet find it difficult to live with myself if I take this route. I could have an overwhelming desire to lose myself in mind-numbing drugs, yet realize that facing my problems is the only way through them.

Alternatively, it might be supposed that my strongest desire should be determined by what motivates me to act. Whatever desire I finally act on is my strongest desire. However, this approach leads to the strange conclusion that I can't really know the strength of my desires until after I have acted. At that point I can say retrospectively which desire was the strongest, but not before. Such an account offers no help at all in assigning a priority structure to various wants that would aid in decision-making. Furthermore, even if I could determine my strongest desire in this sense, it is not what I am looking for. What I am searching for is not the strongest desire, but rather the desire it would be wise to try to satisfy.

The idea that I need to determine my strongest desire reflects a conception of myself as somewhat passive. We can picture various desires as fighting it out in the battlefield of my consciousness, while I observe the battle to determine which one wins. What such a picture leaves out is any active role for me to play in evaluating my desires to determine which are most important for my choices.[3] The kinds of wants that carry real weight in my decisions are those which can be endorsed by my reflective judgment. But how does judgment enter the picture?

One clue which may be of help in prioritizing my wants is to note that desires have a kind of natural structure that is relevant to determining some priorities. This structure arises from the fact that some wants require longer time spans than others for their fulfillment. The desire to travel around the world takes longer to fulfill than the desire to go to the corner to mail a letter. Becoming a concert pianist will require considerably more time than preparing tonight's dinner. The amount of time it takes to fulfill a desire is not always an indication of its importance, but any recognizable human life must maintain some relatively long-term desires, and doing so sets limits on satisfying short-term desires. If I continue to hold getting a college education as a goal, I must structure my activities in such a way as to make the attainment of this goal a realistic possibility.

So part of establishing a priority structure involves deciding what my long-term goals are. Such a decision in effect imposes limits on the short-term goals that may be realistically pursued. For example, deciding to become a successful trial attorney may mean giving up fly-fishing trips during an all-consuming trial. Giving in to the short-term desire to get away from it all might be tempting, but it could undermine effective pursuit of the long-term end. Giving in too many times is one way of giving up the long-term goal.

Recognizing this kind of priority structure need not mean that short-term desires must always give way when they conflict with long-term ends. I might decide that the short-term desire is important enough that I need to pursue my long-term goal in a less effective way, or I might decide that the long-term goal unnecessarily constrains the kind of spontaneity I want my life to exhibit. Short-term goals can rationally be chosen even when they conflict with longer-term goals, but there are limits to our ability to do this and still realistically retain the long-term goal. Hence, a serious commitment to try to achieve a long-term goal is a commitment to make those adjustments in one's life that are needed for effectively pursuing this goal.

PUTTING CHOICES IN PERSPECTIVE

It is possible to think about what I want in various time spans of my life: what I want this day or this year or the next five years. Such thinking can be of some help in structuring daily activities to make it more likely that I will get these wants. Sometimes a little reflection allows me to realize that I am spending inordinate time and effort on things that seem less important when I take into account the big picture. Suppose, however, that we stretch the time span beyond what most people use for strategic planning purposes to encompass our whole life. It makes sense for a person to ask, "What do I want for my life as a whole?" Obviously there is a huge amount of uncertainty in trying to think of life as a whole. We do not know how long our lives may be or what contingencies may shape our future. Nevertheless, there is value in trying to take this perspective. In fact, when we assume this point of view, we discover a way to judge the importance of particular desires and concerns: What is their value in relation to the kind of life we are seeking to construct?

One way to think about our lives as a whole is to reflect on what elements we would like our lives to include. For example, I might decide that I want to visit Paris, or to learn skydiving or to become a Supreme Court Justice. While there is value in thinking about such relatively specific goals and attempting to judge which ones are the most important, my thinking is superficial if all I can do is list particular experiences and achievements I want to be part of my life. My reflection becomes deeper when I can give some account of why the various elements on my list are important. Why do I want to become a Supreme Court Justice? What is it that I think becoming a skydiver will add to my life?

At this level I might determine that each of my goals are ways of realizing certain values I hold. For example, I might value such things as contributing to my community and earning the respect of others. I might place a premium on adventure and discovery or I might care more about security and stability. With some idea of what values concern me most, I can reflect on what ways of achieving these values are crucially important. For example, from the perspective of my life as a whole, I might decide that I definitely want such things as a career that allows me to develop my talents, a strong family life, and a community which will stimulate my intellectual development.[4]

These general characterizations of what I want for my life as a whole help to fill out a perspective from which I can think about the contribution of various particular activities to my overall aims. If I care greatly about having a strong family life, how are my daily pursuits contributing to or taking away from achieving this? If I regard career success as important, am I on a career path that is suited for my talents and interests, and how can I combine the effort I will need in this area with other things I care about?

This sort of reflection can reveal to us our limits. Sometimes people realize too late that they are constantly frustrated by holding images of what they hope to achieve that it is unrealistic to expect to combine. No one can be great in everything, and choosing to pursue a particular way of realizing certain values means implicitly giving up other ways that are equally desirable. Becoming a good judge may mean giving up the goal of becoming a great artist. Having a large family may limit your ability to make a significant impact in community service, at least for a considerable time span.

Because of the limits on what we can realistically expect to combine, reflection on what values are important needs to include some thought about what is essential and what is only desirable. I might be able to live with being only competent in my profession, but find my life a failure if I were merely adequate in raising my children. I might be attracted by an all-consuming passionate relationship, but unwilling to sacrifice a number of close friendships for it. We make such choices implicitly by the way we live, but sometimes we end up with a life that gives up the most important to attain what is only relatively important.

The kind of reflection I am describing here should not be regarded as a once-for-all achievement. People often limit serious reflection on their lives to times of necessity or crisis: when a career choice becomes inevitable, when death or serious illness alters long-established plans, or when failure requires a reorganization of efforts. However, reflection on what sort of life to build is needed even when there is no crisis or forced decision, if we are to get anywhere close to the life we seek. Periodic reevaluations and mid-course corrections are needed to adjust our activities to make sure that there is a firm connection between what we are doing and what we judge important from the perspective of our life as a whole.

It may be misleading to speak of formulating core values and measuring your life in relation to them. For one thing, any attempt to say what is important to you is more like a process in which modification based on experience and further reflection is to be expected. For example, suppose I decide that I value security and predictability. When choosing a career I decide that a way to specify these values is to become an accountant. After working in this field for a while, it becomes apparent that I find this kind of work dull and unfulfilling. This realization might lead me to conclude that I have neglected other important values in my career choice or that I have overstated the importance of security and predictability or that I need to define more precisely what kind of security is important to me.

Or suppose that I have decided that career success is something that is very important to me. I have begun to climb the corporate ladder, focusing on cultivating the right image and doing the kind of work that will be noticed. In the meantime my family life has begun to disintegrate. Realizing that I have undervalued family life, I might reconsider my understanding of career success, thinking about different ways a career could be successful in the light of my awareness of what seeking success of a particular type is likely to produce in my life as a whole.

The thinking process I am trying to describe is complex. It includes (1) trying to say what values I seek to realize in my life as a whole, (2) considering alternative ways to give specific expression to my values, (3) measuring those alternatives according to how well they express my core values and how realistically they can be combined, and (4) revising my values along with my choices of particular activities on the basis of experience and reflection.

Through this type of thinking, I seek to develop a life that I can be pleased with. From the perspective of achieving this end, my desires have a strong claim to satisfaction only to the extent that they can be well-integrated with my conception of a desirable life. I am still trying to get what I want, but I critically judge particular wants in the light of their contribution to what I want for my life as a whole.

SHORTCUTS THAT DON'T WORK

Some philosophers have thought that there must be a simpler and more precise way to do this kind of critical sorting of desires. If we could discover a single thing we are seeking, our ultimate goal, we could measure the contribution of various activities to that goal. The most promising candidate for such a goal is usually thought to be happiness. Each of us is seeking to have a happy life. So our activities might be evaluated on the basis of how much they contribute to or take away from our overall happiness. The problem is that we have no way of doing such an evaluation unless we can make our concept of happiness more specific. If it is spelled out in terms of specific values, like those described in the last section, then the reasoning process to be used is more or less the same.

Suppose, however, that we try to give a more general account of what happiness is by defining it in terms of something we can measure in specific cases. The most influential version of this idea is called hedonism, the view that the values which make a life good can be understood entirely in terms of pleasure and pain. According to the hedonist, whatever is worth seeking is valuable for the pleasure it brings us or the pain it helps us avoid. We may value such things as knowledge or close personal relationships or freedom; but the hedonist claims that the value of each of these is in relation to the pleasure we might gain or the pain we might prevent. According to this view, gaining pleasure and avoiding pain are the ultimate reasons for doing anything.

If we broaden the meaning of the word "pleasure" to include any positive mental experience and the word "pain" to mean any negative mental experience, then we can think of hedonism as the view that what is valuable always comes down to the value of the mental experiences we have. Some hedonists have thought that we could say more precisely what we seek: If we think of mental experiences as if we could assign a positive or negative numerical rating reflecting their value, we want the total of positive numbers to be high and the total of negative numbers to be low. Depending on whether we were more concerned with getting pleasure or with avoiding pain, we can imagine several possible strategies: (1) Act to produce the greatest quantity of pleasure; (2) Act to minimize the amount of pain; or (3) Act to produce the greatest positive score when painful experiences (expressed as negative numbers) are added to pleasurable experiences (expressed as positive numbers). Most hedonists have endorsed the third strategy.

Aside from the problem of actually giving a precise rating to the vast range of particular experiences, hedonism faces a number of strong objections. One is that the general idea that the only things we care about are getting pleasure and avoiding pain is inadequate as an account of what we actually value. If a mother wants her child to have a successful career, does she desire only the pleasure produced by the *belief* that the daughter has been successful or does she want the daughter to actually be successful? If someone could deceive her into thinking that the daughter had achieved success, even though this was false, would that be as much to be desired as the daughter actually being successful? In reality we care about things that transcend our mental reactions to them, valuing states of the world and not just states of mind.

One way to see that our values extend beyond experiences of pleasure and pain is to imagine a thought experiment. Suppose that someone invents a pleasure machine capable of simulating any experience and producing the resultant pleasure for anyone who enters the machine.[5] Also imagine that the machine is able to block off any pain sensations. The machine experience might be comparable to what we call virtual reality. The machine can duplicate any experience that a person wants to have. It is programmed to allow a person to experience such events as climbing Mt. Everest or having a loving relationship or writing a best-selling novel. If some pain is necessary for getting the full pleasure of the experience, we can imagine setting the machine to allow for the appropriate amount of pain.

It is easy to predict that many people might want to give such a machine a try. However, imagine that the inventor of the machine for moral reasons has developed a policy that no one who enters the machine may be removed against his or her will. (The machine is set up in such a way as to maintain a person's bodily functions while he or she is hooked up.) Imagine that there is an exit switch which may be pushed at any time to indicate one's desire to leave. However, up to now, no one has ever pushed the exit switch. Participants have gone from one gratifying experience to another, with no indication of a decision to terminate the activity.

Suppose that knowing all this, you are offered the opportunity to enter the machine. Would you take the opportunity? If pleasure is the only good, it looks as if you should jump at the chance. Perhaps you hesitate because you are worried about other people who may not get the opportunity. In that case let us stipulate that there are enough machines to go around for anyone who wants one. Anyone may enter the machine and experience a life of limitless pleasure. Could there be any reason for hesitating? For many of us I suspect the reason would be a realization of what entering the machine would mean giving up. We could get the pleasure of accomplishments, but not actual accomplishments. We could get the pleasure of having a family, but not a real family. We could experience simulated difficulties to overcome, but no genuine difficulties. We would not be developing our character or helping to build a community or discovering new truths about the world. What the thought experiment reminds us is that some of these other things matter to us as well, perhaps so much that we can imagine giving up a life of pleasure in the machine.

Of course, it is to be expected that some would choose to enter the machine. For some people the alternative might be a life with not much to recommend it. Since some people choose the ultimate escape of suicide, we can certainly imagine that there are those who would choose "machine suicide." But such a choice is a reflection of a real or perceived desperation. Someone with a minimally optimistic assessment of life's possibilities would be less willing to trade them in for the simulated reality provided by the machine.

What about those who are in the machine already? Why do none of them leave? We should probably suspect that there is something addictive about the machine experience. Like rats who are given the opportunity to stimulate the pleasure centers of their brains by pushing a switch and end up lying on the switch until they die, these people are so caught up in the experience that their capacities for reflective judgment have become useless. They have in effect lost the freedom of thought that would be required for pushing the exit switch, and many of us would judge that to be a loss significant enough to outweigh whatever benefit the pleasure machine might offer. It is tempting, but the temptation is to sacrifice too much of what we take to be valuable.

There is another problem with the view that we can reduce all our values to pleasure and pain. It is that when we do so, we are dealing only with isolated experiences, not life as a whole. It is possible to imagine filling your life with pleasurable experiences and minimizing painful experiences, yet having a life which you could not take much satisfaction in. The satisfaction a person is able to get from living a life involves more than compiling pleasure points. At very least the various experiences need to fit together into patterns that express that person's identity. If we are convinced that pleasure is all-important, the preferable approach would be to focus on the question of what kind of life we can take pleasure in, not how much pleasure we can pack into a life.

KNOWLEDGE AND IMAGINATION

If we enter into the hard work of trying to determine what we want out of life, giving up the shortcuts that are more like dead ends, one thing we are bound to discover is that our thinking is going to be limited and fallible. Trying to say what we really value is something that we can only attempt tentatively, with the realization that revision will be necessary and that we need to be open to the possibility of redescribing what we value and rethinking how to express our values in particular activities. Hence, we need a commitment to continue living reflectively, not assuming that we can treat our established patterns as beyond questioning. Of course, reflection too has its limits. It is conceivable that a person could become too reflective for his own good. But for most of us, being too reflective is not the primary problem.

Our attempts to reflect on our lives as a whole are bound to be limited by our knowledge. Sometimes people speak of values as if they were arbitrary preferences that are beyond criticism. However, what we posit as valuable depends to a large extent on what we understand about reality. A person might value fame, aware of some of its benefits, but unaware of its drawbacks. Or someone who thought that a life of simple self-sufficiency, living off the land, would be an improvement over city life, could discover that the idealized life is not all it's cracked up to be. Or one might think that the effects of actions on others is unimportant, due to a failure to understand empathetically the suffering of others. Much of what we do when we try to get straight about what we value is to try to get straight on what the relevant facts are. Improving our knowledge is a key way of improving our values.

To some extent we expect improvement of knowledge to

come from experience. The traditional idea that connects wisdom with age is based in part on the realization that secondhand knowledge may not penetrate as deeply as the kind that a person learns for herself. The idea is not that growing old by itself makes one wise. It is that acquiring experience may be necessary for gaining wisdom. Often, however, one grows older without actually learning much at all from experience. Profiting from experience requires not just reflectiveness, but a willingness to be open to truths that are hard to admit and to adjust beliefs and attitudes in the light of them.

Even though wisdom typically requires reflection on experience, it is a mistake to imagine that the wise person must learn wisdom entirely on her own. Some people gain wisdom by absorbing the teachings of a tradition. Stories and proverbs and traditional practices of a culture may embody a kind of collective wisdom that an individual can tap into. Sometimes the wisdom of the elders is a matter of being keepers and masters of a tradition which contains insight into the value of various ways of living. In our age we find it easy to see that one might slavishly adhere to a tradition rather than using his own critical powers of reflection, but we do not always see the absurdity of thinking that we can discover all we need to know about living on our own.

While there is merit in trying to discover *our own* values, we are only deceiving ourselves if we think that we can individually invent ourselves and create our values from nothing. What we come up with will always owe a debt to the human community that we borrow from whether we realize it or not. In addition our choices of a desirable life depend greatly on the cultural options that are available to us. We may perform limited experiments in living and try to learn from our experiments, but unless we are willing to learn from the collective wisdom of the past, our own thinking is likely to be superficial, and the lessons that we learn may already be well established. In reality, we will selectively use our cultural traditions in formulating our own view of a worthwhile life, even if we are not aware of it. But we are likely to do a better job of this if we realize what we are doing.

Even if we are doubtful about specific ideas from a tradition, we must use a cultural vocabulary with definite meanings as we try to express our own judgments of importance. For example, suppose I decide that I want to have a life with significant accomplishments. I cannot just define for myself what an accomplishment consists in. If my own idea of accomplishment is so idiosyncratic that no one else can understand what it means, I can't meaningfully describe what I aim at as an accomplishment. I need to be able to explicate what I am after in terms of values that others can recognize as values. Rather than thinking of the necessity of using the cultural vocabulary as a limitation, it might be better to think of it as providing the palette of colors from which I am able to paint the picture that is my life.

Thinking about what kind of life to develop is not just an exercise in reasoning; it also calls for imagination. My exploration of the possible ways of realizing my values is limited by my ability to imagine what it might be like to live in various ways. There is no question of trying to imagine all the possible lives anyone might have. I am likely to have enough difficulty even imagining many of the options that are realistically available to me. For instance, if I try to picture what it would be like to become a liberally educated person before beginning the process which may bring this about, my imagination is bound to fall short. The difficulty is in part trying to imagine changes in me that I am not in a position to understand or appreciate until after they have occurred. It is not just that the process will add to my knowledge. It will change the way I think and alter my judgments of what is worth thinking about in ways I cannot fully comprehend in advance.

Of course, I can get some vague idea of what it might be like to develop my life in various directions, and I will usually be aware of people who exhibit the sort of life I am interested in considering. If, for instance, I am thinking about entering a religious monastery, it may be hard to imagine living as a monk, but I can get some understanding from people who are currently living this kind of life before making the commitment myself. Similarly I may have only the vaguest idea of what being a parent means, but parents can give me some idea of what to consider. Nevertheless, there are some things that I won't fully understand except by my own experience. Sometimes the judgment that a particular choice or a particular way of life will satisfy me involves an element of guesswork. Fortunately, there are often halfway measures to enrich my store of experience: I can spend some time in the monastery or keep someone else's children for a week. But such measures do not remove the uncertainty entirely.

Because of the uncertainty of our knowledge and imagination, even the best of planning cannot eliminate the possibility of developing our lives in directions that come to feel like dead ends. While no one can start over entirely, this kind of dissatisfaction can be a significant stimulus to begin to shape your life in new directions. The realization that what you had thought would bring satisfaction has not done so is disappointing, but it may also be an opportunity to reexamine your values to determine whether the dissatisfaction you are feeling reflects the emptiness of your pursuits.

CHOOSING A SELF

When we think about getting what we want, we are apt to imagine satisfying specific and immediate desires, such as the desire for a vacation at the beach or the desire for a promotion. The primary argument of this chapter has been that we need to do some critical sorting to determine which particular desires are worthy of our efforts. The desires that we should attempt to satisfy are those which we can endorse reflectively as fitting into our conception of a desirable life. We may adjust our conception, but it serves as a criterion by which we can weigh our various impulses to determine which ones to endorse and which ones to attempt to ignore or alter.

Judgments about what kind of life to seek and what desires to fulfill are related to the formation of a particular self. When we choose a certain kind of life, we are committing ourselves to become the kind of self who is able to live that life. Just as I cannot become a world-class athlete without building into my character the kind of disciplines necessary to train myself for athletic competition, I cannot live a life devoted to scientific inquiry without building into myself the concerns of a scientist. Imagining a particular type of life involves in part picturing the development of a set of concerns which will shape your perception of the world and your activities. Living that life requires nurturing those concerns and allowing them to shape other desires. The person who has a passion for music and who nurtures this passion by thought and activity can expect to find this passion squeezing out desires which could have shaped the self in alternative directions.

When I ask what kind of life would satisfy me, I am implicitly asking what kind of self I could be satisfied in becoming. However, this raises a problem. Whose satisfaction is being sought? Is it the self that I will be if I take a particular path or the self I am now or some other self? If I am concerned only about my future self, I could develop my life in a direction that might well bring satisfaction to that future self, but would be repugnant to the self I am now. Suppose, for example that I am in a business where shady practices are very common. Right now these practices seem objectionable to me. I find them distasteful and difficult to perform. Suppose I am told by others in the business that they initially had this reaction. However, after engaging in the practices for a few years, they got over their squeamishness and came to actually enjoy the activities. Imagine that there is evidence to predict that if I allow myself to engage in the practices I now deplore, I will get to the point where they don't bother me anymore, and I can be satisfied with my life. Rather than an argument in favor of becoming desensitized to what I now find deplorable, the prospect of later becoming satisfied with myself looks like one I should view with some horror. This kind of satisfaction would be achieved only at the cost of betraying my best reflective judgment now.

So is it the satisfaction of my current self that is the primary concern? That can't be right either. Some possible future lives I could imagine developing would require cultivation of capacities and tastes that I do not now possess. I might find the life of a scholar hopelessly boring, given my present inclinations and capacities, but if my interests and concerns were developed by the right kind of process, this life could be very fulfilling. I cannot use the lack of satisfaction my current self would find with such a life as a basis for judging that life.

But if the satisfaction in question is not that of my current or my future self, then whose could it possibly be? I would suggest that it is the satisfaction of my ideal self, as I can currently conceive it. My conception of the self I aspire to be will include some value judgments which I cannot give up without a fundamental betrayal of myself.[6] They are part of my ideal image which I need to maintain throughout any changes. However, I need to regard my present capacities as limited and subject to possible improvement. The question I face is whether a particular change is something I can judge to be an improvement or something I would need to regard as a regression. To make this judgment I need to bring in my best thinking about what is valuable or important, for what I am trying to determine is whether a particular change would satisfy my aspirations: would it move me closer to or farther from my ideal self? The satisfaction I am looking for is the satisfaction of someone who measures up to my best conception of the self I aspire to become.

When we try to think about our self-interest, we have to think about our desires. However, when we think about satisfying our desires, we face the inevitable question, "Which ones?" For the reflective person the answer is those desires I can integrate well with my conception of a desirable life. A conception of a desirable life will involve judgments of what is worth doing and what qualities are worth developing in a self. Hence, when I start thinking about what I can get for myself, I am drawn to thinking about what I can regard as valuable apart from my own acquisitions. My attempts to pursue self-interested thinking push me in the direction of making a choice of a life and of a self, and this is a choice for which the question, "What is in my self-interest?" yields no answer. I need to engage in a different kind of thinking before my self-interested thinking can get off the ground.

Chapter Four

DEALING WITH WHAT YOU DON'T WANT

So I boiled with anger, sighed, wept, and was at my wits' end. I found no calmness, no capacity for deliberation.... Everything was an object of horror, even light itself; all that was not he made me feel sick and was repulsive—except for groaning and tears. In them alone was there some slight relief. But when my weeping stopped, my soul felt burdened by a vast load of misery.... I had become to myself a place of unhappiness in which I could not bear to be; but I could not escape from myself. (Augustine[1])

The way in which a man accepts his fate and all the suffering it entails...gives him ample opportunity—even under the most difficult circumstances—to add a deeper meaning to his life.... Here lies the chance for a man either to make use of or forgo the opportunities for attaining moral values that a difficult situation may afford him. And this decides whether he is worthy of his suffering or not. (Victor Frankl[2])

A story from the ancient Near East tells of a servant who one morning in the marketplace saw a figure, whom he recognized as Death, gesturing towards him. Frightened, the servant ran to his master and pleaded, "Master, please lend me your fastest horse. Death has picked me out, and I must flee from him to Baghdad." With the master's consent, the servant made his escape. Later that day the master had occasion to go into the marketplace where he too saw the one who had frightened his servant. Approaching Death, the master said, "Why did you alarm my servant today by pointing at him menacingly?" Death replied, "I did not mean to frighten your servant, but I was surprised to see him here, since I have an appointment to meet him this evening in Baghdad."

The story illustrates a persistent idea that is usually called fatalism, the view that certain particular events are bound to occur regardless of how we try to avoid them. According to this idea, our struggle against the inevitable will only succeed in helping to bring it about. Most of us are not fatalists, but even if we doubt that particular future events are destined to occur, we have to admit that our control over the future is limited. Even if the servant in the story is able to avoid death on some particular day, he cannot expect to escape it indefinitely. Similarly, no matter how skillful we are at avoiding undesirable events, we will inevitably be confronted by some occurrences that we would not have chosen. Disease, natural disasters, death of loved ones, betrayal, and failure can come into our lives despite the best of precautions. Part of thinking about our self-interest is deciding how to deal with the unwanted eventualities that we will face.

The idea that we can do much to prepare for those unpleasant experiences that we would very much like to avoid may sound far-fetched. However, it is pretty clear that the extent to which we suffer from unwelcome occurrences depends not just on what happens, but on the attitudes that we have toward what happens. If we cannot always prevent the things we regard as negative, perhaps we can alter our attitudes toward them so that they don't disturb us as much. If we cannot always achieve what we seek, perhaps we can adopt attitudes that will not leave us feeling so disappointed at failure. While there is wisdom in this idea, I will argue in this chapter that some programs of attitude-modification go overboard. Ultimately I will opt for a moderate program of self-adjustment.

ADJUSTING OURSELVES

An extreme version of the view that the key to good living is to be found in adopting the proper attitudes is presented in the writings of the Roman Stoic, Epictetus. Epictetus attempts to show us the attitudes we need, using a distinction between what is under our control and what is not under our control.[3] Included in the latter category are such things as honors, wealth, health, reputation, professional achievements, and personal relationships. In classifying these things as beyond our control, Epictetus is not saying that our actions have no effect on whether we are healthy or whether we have friends. Rather he is saying that we cannot guarantee gaining or keeping any of these things. Fatal disease may strike the person with the best of health habits. Loved ones may die or they may betray the most loyal and trustworthy of companions. Thieves may take away cherished possessions, or totalitarian governments may confiscate them. If we put our hopes in any of these attainments, we may be disappointed despite our best efforts. Ultimately these things are not under our control.

It might seem as if Epictetus is being overly pessimistic, but his point is that underlying our suffering are exaggerated expectations about what is under our control. If we can scale back our expectations to a more reasonable level, we will find ourselves better adjusted to reality. The kind of adjustment Epictetus thinks we need becomes clear when we see what he regards as under our control. Here he lists our thoughts, our choices, our desires, and our purposes. Epictetus sometimes refers to what is beyond our control as externals. Under our control are those things which are internal to our minds.

So the idea is that while you cannot control whether you will have wealth, you can, by adopting the right kind of attitudes, have contentment even if poverty should be your lot. You can't control what other people think of you or what they do to you. They may spread false stories about you or they may accuse you unjustly and have you thrown in jail. Regardless of what they do, thinks Epictetus, you have control over your own reaction. Ultimately you decide whether you let these events make you bitter and vengeful or whether you preserve your own peace of mind. Epictetus wants us to deal with our lack of control over externals by magnifying our control over our thoughts and attitudes. How are we supposed to achieve this control?

Epictetus suggests a program of desire modification. He says,

> ...if you try to avoid disease, or death, or poverty, you will experience misfortune. Withdraw, therefore, your aversion from all the matters that are not under our control...remove utterly your desire; for if you desire some one of the things that are not under our control you are bound to be unfortunate..." (#2, p. 485)

The prescription is a radical one. Since we cannot always be sure that our desires will be satisfied, we are to change our desires so that we only desire what we can be sure of getting. If you can get rid of your desire to avoid disease, disgrace, friendlessness, or whatever is out of your control, you will be able to receive these events with tranquility of mind. Since you cannot be sure of preventing these events and you can control your reaction to them, you should concentrate your efforts on modifying your desires to conform to the events. Epictetus sums up the goal as follows: "Do not seek to have everything that happens happen as you wish, but wish for everything to happen as it actually does happen, and your life will be serene." (#8, p. 491) Our serenity is disturbed when reality does not conform to our desires, so when we cannot control reality, we are to concentrate our efforts on adjusting our desires.

Clearly the kind of modification called for is a major one. What needs to be cultivated is a kind of indifference to anything I might lose. I must not care whether I am successful, whether my ideas influence others, whether I live in a nice house, or whether I fall victim to a debilitating disease. I must have no desires to avoid anything that might actually happen. If I desire certain events not to occur, I may be alarmed when these events come my way, but if I do not have a desire for anything beyond my control, then I can be content with whatever happens.

How does Epictetus expect to produce the appropriate desire modification? Essentially it is a matter of learning to get rid of thought patterns which are conducive to inordinate desires. For example, Epictetus urges us to cease viewing what we have as possessions. If we think that something belongs to us, it will be disturbing if it is taken away. However, if we think of each thing as loaned to us temporarily, it should not be disturbing when it is recalled. Epictetus applies this, not just to property, but to anything we might imagine ourselves to possess. He urges, "Never say about anything 'I have lost it,' but only 'I have given it back.' Is your child dead? It has been given back. Is your wife dead? It has been given back." (#11, p. 491) The idea Epictetus is promoting might sound callous, particularly if we imagine him speaking these words to a grieving parent or spouse. However, he is attempting to remind us as human beings of our place in the scheme of things. We should think of life and death as matters beyond our control. Epictetus personally thought of such things as being in God's hands. But whether we think of that which takes away what is now in our keeping as acts of God or as products of an impersonal order, the realization that loss is possible should lead us, thinks Epictetus, not to hold on too tightly to what we might have to relinquish.

One of the images Epictetus uses to illustrate the appropriate attitude is that of a banquet. When various dishes are passed to you, you may reach out and take a portion, but you should neither anticipate what is expected to come round, nor lament missing something that has already gone by. Enjoy what you are given at the present time without becoming attached to it. (#15, p. 495)

In a related image Epictetus pictures life as a sea voyage. The ship has temporarily anchored and you are allowed to explore the beach. You may pick up some shell fish or some plants during your exploration, but don't get so caught up in these things that you miss the Captain's call to return to the ship. Epictetus is warning us not to become too attached to the possessions and the relationships of life. Given the possibility that we may have to give them up, we should not regard them as essential to our happiness or security.

The idea of nonattachment is developed by Epictetus through his suggestion that we adopt a kind of external perspective on things. He says at one point that we should apply to our own lives the attitudes we typically take toward others' lives: When someone else has suffered some loss, we may think to ourselves that this is the kind of thing to be expected in a world like ours. Yet when our own child has died, the sense of loss may be nearly intolerable. Epictetus thinks that remembering our response when the event happened to strangers can give us a critical distance from violent and unpleasant emotions. By viewing our own lives from an external, somewhat detached perspective, we can let go of the weight of grief.

What we are aware of from this external perspective is in large measure the contingency of human existence. Things get lost or stolen. People unexpectedly get sick and die. Plans for the future are destroyed by the choices of others. All these things we know. But we are apt to forget them when we get caught up in our own plans and projects. Epictetus suggests constantly reminding ourselves of the ways we can be disappointed. For example, he urges someone about to go to the public baths to think of the bad things that happen in such places: people splash you and jostle you and even rob you. (#4, p. 487) Keeping these predictable negatives in mind enables us to avoid overly optimistic expectations. Forming unrealistic ideas of what is likely is a good way to set ourselves up for disappointment.

Applying this idea to someone who wants to enter the Olympics, Epictetus urges careful reflection on the hardships that can be realistically expected:

> Do you wish to win an Olympic victory? So do I, by the gods! for it is a fine thing. But consider the matters which come before that...You have to submit to discipline, follow a strict diet, give up sweet cakes, train under compulsion, at a fixed hour, in heat or in cold; you must not drink cold water, nor wine just whenever you feel like it;...Then when the contest comes on, you have to "dig in" beside your opponent, and sometimes dislocate your wrist, sprain your ankle, swallow quantities of sand, sometimes take a scourging and along with all that get beaten. (#29, p. 507)

After you have all this clearly in your mind, you are ready to make the choice, but not until you have a realistic idea of the costs.

For Epictetus such pessimistic reminders are not just for those engaged in particularly challenging pursuits. We are to continually keep before our imaginations the worst outcomes to keep our ambitions under control. He teaches,

> Keep before your eyes day by day death and exile, and everything that seems terrible, but most of all death; and then you will never have any abject thought, nor will you yearn for anything beyond measure. (#21, p. 499)

Such gloomy advice is a hard pill to swallow, but Epictetus thinks that this kind of discipline is absolutely necessary, if we are to keep our desires in check. If we let ourselves, we can drift into all kinds of rosy expectations which inevitably lead to frustration and disappointment.

Epictetus teaches that it is not the events of life that drive us to despair. It is the judgments that we make about these events. When we understand the difference between what we control and what is beyond our control, Epictetus thinks we will understand the wisdom in reserving judgments of good and bad for what is under our control. If we can accept external events as expressions of the order of things and recognize that order is beyond our control, we won't spend so much futile effort resisting and second-guessing what we cannot change. We can instead direct our efforts towards developing the attitudes which will enable us to live a satisfying life.

THE LIMITS OF INVULNERABILITY

What Epictetus seeks is an area of invulnerability where an individual can be completely secure against any kind of threat to a good life.[4] His distinction between what we can control and what we cannot control is based on the assumption that only total control would count as any kind of control. In his thought, if you could be 95 percent sure that the government is not going to send you to prison for twenty years, that would not be enough to preserve your peace of mind against this possibility. There is always a chance that this unlikely event will come about, and if your happiness rests on remaining free, then you are not completely secure.

However, the kind of security Epictetus wants does not come

without costs. To gain the sort of inner tranquility he thinks necessary for good living we would have to give up some things that many people assume are needed for a desirable life. Consider, for example, Epictetus' advice about losing a wife. He wants us to cultivate the kind of attitude where the death is not contrary to any desire. But to have such an attitude is precisely to have no deep attachment at all. Whatever kind of enjoyment one could get from being with a spouse without wanting the relationship to continue is a far cry from what we ordinarily call the experience of love. By cultivating this sort of detachment, we might gain a kind of security, but it comes at the cost of living a solitary existence.

Not only would this strategy undercut personal relationships. It would deprive us of much of the passion needed for pursuing any difficult or challenging path. If you are to be indifferent about whether you become a physician, can you still muster the effort to study long hours and go through the rigors of internship? If you must only want things in the kind of detached way of being able to easily take them or leave them, you must renounce the kind of motivation that keeps us striving after dreams that we deeply care about.

Epictetus advises at one point, "You can be invincible if you never enter a contest in which victory is not under your control." (#19, p. 497) Quite so, but isn't there some value in investing your energies in goals that are far from sure things? Epictetus' strategy is designed to help us avoid disappointment, but what he is urging is a kind of play-it-safe existence that elevates self-protection above any other kind of value. However, in renouncing risks, we are also renouncing the possibility of achieving the kinds of things that are inherently risky. Even if we could be sure of insulating ourselves against disappointments in this way, we do so only by narrowing our vision of life's possibilities. We avoid defeat by refusing to enter into the battles through which we might have achieved victories.

If we are reluctant to accept Epictetus' advice, it may be because we do not share his conception of a good life. Epictetus' fundamental value is what we might call contentment: the absence of frustrated desires. If contentment is what we are seeking, then the strategy of cutting back on desires that may not be satisfied is entirely reasonable. Admittedly, Epictetus goes to the extreme by seeking to cut back our desires to the point where we have no risk of disappointment, but we should certainly recognize that people often create their own misery by hanging onto some desires long after it is evident that there is no realistic chance of satisfying them. We can often increase our level of contentment by modifying some desires in the light of reality.

However, contentment is not the only thing we value. It is possible to imagine someone who is very contented with life, but suffers from an extreme poverty of aspirations. Suppose I build a whole life around playing video games. When I am playing, I am content. Everything else I must do, such as eating or sleeping or interacting with any people, is accepted as the price I must pay to play more video games. It is only the games that give me any satisfactions, and it is the games I live for. If on the whole I am able to achieve a high degree of contentment, does that mean I am living a desirable life? Does it mean that my life wouldn't be improved by developing a broader range of aspirations?

Most of us want more than contentment. We seek a broad range of experiences and activities that we can judge to be worthwhile. While limited abilities or a restricted range of opportunities may narrow our vision of life's possibilities, we can still recognize it as a failure or a temptation to become contented too easily without developing our abilities or accepting some difficult challenges. Contentment is a value, but it is not the only ingredient that is needed for building a desirable life. In fact, sometimes we can recognize values that are worth including in a life that we can only expect to attain at the cost of giving up some contentment.

Knowledge is one such value. People who get a liberal education usually say that the process has improved their lives. But the improvement does not necessarily mean that they are more content. Ideas can be disturbing, and being changed from a person who finds a narrow and dogmatic perspective obvious to one who understands a variety of perspectives and sees more ambiguity in some issues, may mean a good deal less contentment. A conception of a good life that includes educational development might lead us to judge a life with such development to be better over all, even though that life contained an increased amount of dissatisfaction.[5]

Epictetus goes wrong, I think, in focusing on our satisfaction or lack of satisfaction with particular events. It is possible for a satisfying life to contain a great many unsatisfying elements, and decreasing the number of unsatisfying elements does not always improve the overall quality of the life. What is crucial is not whether we are pleased with all the elements in our life, but being satisfied with the overall shape of the life we are living and the person we are becoming. Whether or not a particular desire should be modified depends on how that modification might fit in or fail to fit in with the kind of life one is seeking to build.

For example, if my conception of a desirable life includes deep attachments and loving relationships, I definitely do not want to embark on the kind of desire-modification program that Epictetus advocates. Even if I knew that the program would be successful and that it would make me more content, it would take away something which is fundamental to the kind of life I want to have. My conception of a good life involves the risk of significant loss and grief, but that risk is the price I must pay for a life rich in relational values.

While it is undoubtedly correct that we do not want our efforts at achieving a good life to be spoiled by adversity, we do not need to be so insulated from potentially negative experiences that they leave us completely unaffected. We do need to be able to respond to experiences which cause us grief in ways that allow us to continue regarding our lives as worthwhile. But it is possible for a person to accept a great many frustrations as part of a worthwhile life. Indeed it is possible to see great value in how one responds to events which disrupt cherished plans and hopes.

FACING ADVERSITY

Victor Frankl's life was changed irrevocably when he entered a

Nazi concentration camp during World War II. Frankl, who had been a prominent psychiatrist, found his identity reduced to the number that had been tattooed on his skin. He was stripped of every possession, including the manuscript that had been his life's work, which he futilely tried to save. Separated from his family, Frankl learned after the war that only a single sister had survived. His father, mother, brother and wife died in the camps or were exterminated in the gas ovens.

In the concentration camp each day became a struggle to survive the periodic selection processes that sent prisoners still capable of heavy labor in one direction and those too sick or feeble to the crematoriums. Frankl, along with the other prisoners, received a starvation diet of watery soup and a little bread. He marched to the work site each day with clothing that had become rags and shoes that hardly fit over his swollen and aching feet. Working in the freezing weather, Frankl endured the blows and insults of sadistic guards, only to come back each night to appalling and overcrowded barracks where typhus epidemics were routine. In such hellish conditions a few hours sleep could seem like a luxury.

Frankl tells of an incident in which a fellow prisoner was having a horrible nightmare. He started to wake the man up. Then he stopped:

> Suddenly I drew back the hand which was ready to shake him, frightened at the thing I was ready to do. At that moment I became intensely conscious of the fact that no dream, no matter how horrible, could be as bad as the reality of the camp which surrounded us, and to which I was about to recall him. (p. 28)

In these disgusting and dehumanizing conditions the prisoners tried to endure, clinging to the wildly improbable hope of survival and release.

In describing factors that enabled people to endure, Frankl mentions the value of being able to retreat into the inner world of the mind. Prisoners who had a rich intellectual life were able to tap their inner resources, often surviving better than more physically robust individuals without such development. Frankl tells of a march in which he was able to shut out the harsh surroundings by dwelling on thoughts of his wife. Even though he did not know whether she was alive or dead, he was able to experience moments akin to bliss in the contemplation of one he loved.

However, the crucial factor in being able to endure, according to Frankl, is to be found in the attitudes prisoners adopted toward their suffering. He writes,

> What was really needed was a fundamental change in our attitude toward life. We had to learn ourselves and, furthermore, we had to teach the despairing men, that it did not really matter what we expected from life, but rather what life expected from us.... Life ultimately means taking the responsibility to find the right answer to its problems and to fulfill the task which it constantly sets for each individual. (p. 77)

Like Epictetus, Frankl is urging a kind of adjustment in attitude. But the adjustment he calls for is not an attempt to avoid unsatisfying experiences by getting rid of desires for anything other than what occurs. The prisoners who are persuaded by Frankl can still regard their circumstances as miserable and their imprisonment as unjust and evil. However, they are to think of the evil as a challenging opportunity to show what they are made of. They would have avoided this suffering if they could have, but since it has been thrust upon them, they are to regard it as their task and to face up to it with all the dignity and inner strength they can find.

Rather than despairing about all they have lost, Frankl is urging his fellow prisoners to focus on what they will do. Instead of thinking of themselves as powerless victims, they are to think of themselves as active agents who can choose how to respond to their suffering. He says,

> The way in which a man accepts his fate and all the suffering it entails, the way in which he takes up his cross, gives

> him ample opportunity—even under the most difficult circumstances—to add a deeper meaning to his life. It may remain brave, dignified and unselfish. Or in the bitter fight for self-preservation he may forget his human dignity and become no more than an animal. Here lies the chance for a man either to make use of or to forgo the opportunities of attaining the moral values that a difficult and demanding situation may afford him. And this decides whether he is worthy of his sufferings or not. (p. 67)

The idea that we can be or fail to be worthy of our sufferings presupposes an ideal of human life that places great importance on an individual's capacity to express her identity by free choices. The person without a secure hold on who she is and what she stands for faces a strong temptation in hardship to give in to despair. Frankl says of prisoners who lost their hold on life, "...they did not take their life seriously and despised it as something of no consequence." (p. 78)

By contrast the people who were able to deal with their sufferings were those who could see their response to this difficult situation as a vitally important revelation of their character. The circumstances were putting them to the test, and it was in their power to respond well or badly. As he puts it,

> Once the meaning of suffering had been revealed to us, we refused to minimize or alleviate the camp's tortures by ignoring them or harboring false illusions and entertaining optimism. Suffering had become a task on which we did not want to turn our backs. We had realized its hidden opportunities for achievement...Therefore it was necessary to face up to the full amount of suffering....(p. 78)

The point is not to make the suffering any worse, and it is certainly not to seek out unnecessary suffering. It is to insist upon exercising freedom to preserve one's fundamental values in the face of suffering.

Fortunately, most of us will not have to face the extreme deprivations of the concentration camp. Even so, we cannot expect to go through life unscathed. Life is risky, and each of us can expect our share of anguishing experiences. Epictetus speaks to us about how to protect ourselves against disappointment; Frankl speaks to us about accepting the disappointments that are a part of living and making the most of a bad situation.

Sometimes people's lives are wrecked by circumstances far less severe than life in a concentration camp. The death of a child, divorce, financial catastrophe, public disgrace, or physical disability can be terrible experiences which drive a person to despair, sometimes never to recover. When you have invested your energies and your hopes in something that collapses before your eyes, finding the heart to continue can be difficult. We admire those people who are able to respond to tragedy with dignity and courage, but the task of rebuilding from the materials that are left over can seem overwhelming.

When adversity strikes, we need a conception of the kind of life we want and the kind of self we aspire to be that is resilient enough to withstand the collapse of our hopes and dreams. Reality continually forces us to adjust our aims, but through all the necessary adjustments, we need a character that is sturdy enough to enable us to preserve that which we hold fundamentally important. Difficult circumstances may call for limited aspirations and lowered expectations, but our attempts to cope with reality need to be guided by a sense of identity that doesn't change with the weather.

In ancient Athens Socrates was sentenced to death for pursuing a life that he regarded as a God-given mission. As he saw it, his task in life was to examine his own and other people's values, urging each person to be most concerned with the "improvement of the soul" rather than with external attainments, such as money or popular acclaim. Socrates tells the jury that he will not give up the kind of life he has been living even if death is the result. After receiving the death sentence, Socrates makes a remarkable claim. He says, "...no evil can happen to a good man..."[6]

Socrates is not denying that a person might suffer financial losses or debilitating illness or even unjust execution. He is saying that the evil we should fear is the corruption of the soul, or as we might say, the loss of the self. This loss, thinks Socrates, is not something that happens to us—it comes about only when we consent to it by our choices. While we may not be able to avoid adverse circumstances, we can preserve our integrity by responding to these circumstances in a way consistent with our fundamental values. Socrates does not mean to suggest that this is easy. On the contrary, there are great pressures to give in and conform to what others are expecting or to avoid suffering by taking moral shortcuts. It takes considerable inner strength to withstand the pressures.

OPTIMIZING AND ADAPTING

The question of how to deal with the troubles that life thrusts upon us has been a central concern of philosophical and religious thinkers since ancient times. Steven Luper classifies the basic strategies into two types.[7] One he calls optimizing, the strategy of taking our desires for granted and looking for ways to satisfy them efficiently. Luper regards optimizing as the standard Western approach. The alternative strategy he calls adapting, altering our desires to bring them into greater conformity with reality. Adapting is the characteristic Eastern approach found in thinkers such as Gautama Buddha and Lao Tzu. It is also found in Western schools of thought such as Stoicism and Epicureanism.

The most extreme form of adapting is the attempt to transform oneself into the kind of person who has no desires that will be unsatisfied. Epictetus' attempt to make us invulnerable to the events of life is an example of this extreme. What I have suggested is a less extreme form of adapting, involving a critical evaluation of desires in terms of their contribution to one's overall conception of a desirable life within the limits set by the expected demands of reality. Sometimes it is wise to scale back our desires, and as we reflect on what we want for our lives as a whole, we are often able to see how diminishing particular desires can make it more likely that we will achieve the kind of life we want.

There is considerable contemporary psychological research to indicate that, within certain limits, life-satisfaction has less to do with our objective circumstances than with our response to the circumstances we face. People whose lives are radically altered by some piece of good fortune (say, winning the lottery) are initially elated, but within a relatively short period of time, their level of happiness tends to approximate what it was before. Similarly, people who experience great tragedy, such as becoming blind or paralyzed, after a period of adjustment, typically return to their previous level of happiness.[8] The most plausible explanation for this surprising result is that people's level of satisfaction is closely related to their expectations. After a change in circumstances people tend to adjust their baseline of expectations up or down so that it may take much more or much less to produce happiness. When our expectations are drastically reduced, we may discover greater appreciation for the small pleasures that we previously took for granted.

In the light of this result we should be able to recognize the wisdom of the ancient idea that learning to cherish the simple pleasures of life—a quiet walk, a conversation with a friend, a sunset—may do more for our level of satisfaction than pinning our hopes on fulfilling an ever-expanding set of desires for more and more. If we could learn to enjoy life's opportunities without being possessed by them, we would be better prepared to make the most of the good which does come our way. While I have argued that the extreme kind of adjustment in attitude that Epictetus advocates is not desirable, he is on the right track in thinking that the key to good living is not in giving our desires free rein, but in modifying our attitudes and desires so that we may expand our capacity for contentment even in potentially frustrating circumstances.

Desire modification is an important feature of human life. The typical grief process in which one moves from denial to acceptance is a kind of desire modification produced by the need to face up to reality. But in addition to modifications which are more or less forced upon us, we can sometimes consciously undertake to alter desires that we recognize as unproductive sources of frustration. As thinkers such as Epictetus make clear, our desires depend on our thoughts. We may not be able to modify a desire at will, but ceasing to think in ways that fuel a desire is an important tool for adjusting it. The wife who becomes convinced that her unfaithful and abusive spouse will never change may still have the desire to remain with him, but by dwelling on what she knows to be true and refusing to entertain comforting but unrealistic hopes, she stands a good chance of modifying that desire.

Facing up to adversity requires us to adjust our desires to a reality that is sometimes harsh. However, our adjustment needs to be tempered by our aspirations. In difficult circumstances the kind of life we had wanted and expected may no longer be possible. Usually, however, we can still think about what it is possible to salvage of our self-image and our sense of what is worthwhile, even in trying conditions. The kind of life we choose in conditions of adversity will undoubtedly differ from what we would have chosen, given greater opportunities. But, as Frankl makes clear, there is opportunity for giving expression to values fundamental to our identity even under very difficult conditions.

THE PURSUIT OF SELF-INTEREST

In Part One I have attempted to show that self-interested thinking needs to be guided by a conception of a desirable life and a conception of the kind of self needed to live that life. It is easy to get caught up in measuring individual gains or losses in a way that makes the pursuit of self-interest lose its point. However, our thinking about how to benefit ourselves can serve our purposes when it is regulated by reflection on the self we aspire to develop. Part Two focuses on the issue of choosing a particular self from among the available options.

Part Two

CHOOSING A SELF

Who am I then? Tell me that first, and then, if I like being that person, I'll come up: if not, I'll stay down here till I'm somebody else… (Alice in Lewis Carroll's *Alice's Adventures in Wonderland*[1])

…so the richest personality is nothing before he has chosen himself; and on the other hand even what might be called the poorest personality is everything when he has chosen himself, for the greatness is not to be this or that but to be oneself, and every human being can be this if he so wills it. (Judge Wilhelm in Kierkegaard's *Either/Or*[2])

PRELUDE TO PART TWO

Suggesting that we have a capacity to choose a self sounds odd. Most people treat the self as a given, rather than something one might intentionally mold or create. There may be a sense in which each of us can be said to choose the self we have become, but for many of us this is the sense in which failing to decide something can amount to a decision. One who gives neither thought nor effort to overcoming slothful tendencies thereby "decides" to remain a slothful person. But this way of making a decision may be distinguished from the kind of choice made by one who thoughtfully considers the available options and seeks to make one of them real.

Part Two is about consciously considering the selves one might become and choosing to identify with one of the many possibilities. In contrast to self-interested thinking which involves weighing potential benefits of alternative actions to determine which is the most beneficial, thinking about choosing a self involves a reflective consideration of alternative ways of life. One who engages in this mode of thought is trying to formulate aspirations for the self that express her most considered judgments of value and to discover how those aspirations apply to her own situation. Each of the chapters in this section takes a particular range of options with regard to self-formation and attempts to stimulate the reader to reflect on this range in relation to his or her own life.

Chapter Five considers the possibility of building into the self concerns for other people. Expanding the self in this way makes possible goods such as friendship and love which many people would judge as crucial to a desirable life. However, gaining these goods means becoming a self who is motivated to act on the basis of concerns for things other than its own benefit. From the perspective of a self who cares about no one else, there may be no compelling reason to develop such concerns. However, one who has some understanding of the way of life that expansion of the self makes possible may have powerful reasons for developing and preserving the capacities for this way of life.

Another way to alter the self is through limits or restrictions. All of us have to deal with external restrictions on the pursuit of our goals. However, for many people the force of moral restrictions is an internal one. Chapter Six examines the choice to develop or maintain a self with built-in limits on the pursuit of its goals. From one point of view, intentionally developing such a self seems rationally unintelligible. However, anyone who genuinely cares about the well-being of others has reason to want to treat them with a respect that implicitly calls for limits. Also, choosing not to internalize moral limits means living with a considerable gap between public persona and private self. Furthermore, some of the self-images a person might have good reason to aspire to involve built-in limits.

Chapter Seven discusses modifications of the self that involve developing some human capacity such as intellectual development or development of artistic sensitivities or social skills. When we contemplate the various possibilities, we often have only a dim awareness of what a particular form of development would mean. We rely on imaginative constructions based on exemplars we have encountered or experiences that suggest the possibility of a better way of life. Since development often involves a change of one's interests, desires, and values, it is hard to compare what we might become with what we are. However, sometimes we become convinced that a particular type of development would be an improvement and is suited to our individual inclinations and aspirations.

Chapter Eight focuses on the problem of becoming a self who is engaged in doing things that he or she can reflectively judge to be worthwhile. Our reflective capacities allow us to evaluate our activities, judging what we do in terms of various value concepts (e.g., meaningful, empty, noble, disgusting, etc.), and these reflective valuations represent a perspective wider than the self. By building into the self concerns that resonate with our reflective valuations, we make possible the kinds of engagements that contribute to a life we can regard as satisfying. While this sort of development is potentially costly, so is a policy of suppressing our reflective aspirations.

In each of this section's chapters it becomes apparent that choosing to become a particular kind of self alters one's self-interest. When self-interested thinking is applied to the kind of self one has reflectively chosen to become, judgments about what actions are beneficial will be relative to the concerns and constraints that self aspires to have. Furthermore, this section also illustrates how our reflective thinking may lead us to seek to become a self who is motivated by things other than self-interest. To fulfill our aspirations, we may need to acquire and nurture concerns that extend beyond personal benefit. The point of this section is not to make the reflective choice of a self for anyone. That would surely be an impossible task. Instead it is to stimulate your reflection in ways that are relevant to formulating a conception of life that satisfies your own most considered judgments of value.

Chapter Five

THE EXPANDED SELF

When people who are tolerably fortunate in their outward lot do not find in life sufficient enjoyment to make it valuable to them, the cause generally is caring for nobody but themselves. (John Stuart Mill[1])

... there is no imprudence more flagrant than that of Selfishness in the ordinary sense of the term,--that excessive concentration of attention on the individual's own happiness which renders it impossible for him to feel any strong interest in the pleasures and pains of others. The perpetual prominence of self that hence results tends to deprive all enjoyments of their keenness and zest, and produce rapid satiety and *ennui*... (Henry Sidgwick[2])

The film, *Groundhog Day*, is a fable for our time.[3] The story centers around Phil, an egotistical weatherman for a local television station, whose world is defined by his self-centered preoccupations. Phil is assigned by his station to cover the annual celebration of Groundhog Day in Punxsutawney, Pennsylvania. Regarding this assignment as beneath him and the small-town community as unworthy of his attention, Phil grudgingly accompanies an assistant producer (Rita) and a cameraman (Larry) on the trip.

Phil's interactions with his coworkers reveal an arrogant sense of his own importance. He is rude, sarcastic, and condescending when he addresses them; he refers to himself as "the talent." Such behavior is consistent with his attitude toward people in general. "People are morons," he says. He treats virtually everyone with a thinly veiled contempt, confident of his own superiority over the foolish masses.

After the Groundhog Day festivities Phil is eager to get out of town as quickly as possible. However, an unexpected blizzard forces the television crew to return and spend another night. Waking up the next morning to a repeat of the previous day's music and radio chatter, Phil comes eventually to realize that it is Groundhog Day again. On subsequent days the strange time loop continues, forcing Phil to repeat the same day over and over. Only Phil is aware that he is living multiple versions of the same day. Each day he will pass the homeless man, meet the obnoxious high school classmate who has become an insurance agent, and deliver his television spiel about Groundhog Day. He knows in advance what other people will do and what they will say, unless he alters his own behavior.

At first, reliving the same day seems like a nightmare. Phil goes for a head x-ray and then visits a psychiatrist; neither is any help. In time, however, Phil begins to see the possibilities. If there is no tomorrow, there are no consequences to be feared. He can do whatever strikes his fancy, breaking all the rules without risking any lasting suffering. So Phil eats gluttonously, smokes, drives on the railroad tracks, pursuing his urges without any concern for the long term. He is not entirely impulsive, however. Sometimes he plans gratifications for the following day. Since he will be living the same day over, he can use information gathered on one day to achieve what he seeks when the events are replayed. For example, he observes the carelessness of the armored truck drivers on one day and walks off with a bag of money the next. He learns enough about the woman he meets one day to be effective in his subsequent seduction attempt. He learns all the answers on *Jeopardy* and later impresses others with his knowledge. If anything goes wrong, such as being arrested and put in jail, he can count on waking up safely in his own bed the next morning for the beginning of another Groundhog Day.

Eventually Phil goes after a more challenging gratification. He seeks to take his assistant producer, Rita, to bed. Phil goes about the task systematically. Each day he acquires information about Rita, her likes and dislikes, and particularly what qualities she is attracted to in a man. Given infinite time, he can correct any missteps of the previous day to make their interactions go better. When he learns that her college major focused on nineteenth-century French poetry, he is able to take the time to memorize a poem and quote it to her in French when he replays their encounter. All of this effort culminates in the creation of several nearly perfect days, but each time Phil seeks to cap off the romantic day with a sexual encounter, he is rebuffed. His efforts degenerate into frenetic imitations of his earlier actions, and he is plunged into deep depression.

Despairing of life, Phil tries to kill himself by various methods. He drives off a cliff, puts an electric toaster in his bathtub, steps in front of a truck, and jumps from a tall building. None of these methods succeeds. Each time he wakes up safely in bed the next morning to begin another Groundhog Day.

One day Phil confides his plight to Rita. He convinces her of the truth of his account by displaying his godlike knowledge of all the people in the diner and of what will happen next, such as the waiter dropping a tray of dishes exactly on cue. As Phil and Rita spend the day together, Phil is drawn towards her. He becomes aware of her kindness and her caring responses, and he is pulled out of himself enough to fall in love with her. While she is sleeping, he says to her, "If ever I could, I swear I would love you for the rest of my life."

That day is the beginning of a new Phil. He realizes that living the same day over does not have to be a curse. It can be an opportunity to change his way of living. With this new perspective, Phil begins to look around for how he can make a positive difference. Initially, he spends a whole day trying to save the life of a homeless man. When this effort is unsuccessful, he investigates to find other tragedies he might prevent. In addition to devoting himself to helping other people, Phil also begins to work on improving himself. He takes piano lessons, learns ice sculpture, and reads great literature.

Soon we are shown what all this effort has produced. Phil's day begins with a poetic tribute to the people of Punxsutawney, whom he had formerly despised. He spends the day occupied with such activities as rescuing a boy who falls out of a tree, changing a flat tire for several old ladies, using the Heimlich maneuver to save a choking man. After a day of good deeds, Phil entertains the people of the town by playing the piano at an evening party. Rita observes strangers, one after another, thanking Phil for some helpful act. Impressed, she "buys" him at the charity auction. Phil is a changed man, and to the new Phil, Rita responds wholeheartedly with her love. The next morning when Phil wakes up, it is the day after Groundhog Day, and he makes plans to settle down with Rita in Punxsutawney.

PHIL'S TRANSFORMATION

The meaning of the fable is not difficult to discern. What seems to Phil at one point to be a terrible punishment is actually an opportunity to begin again. He must live the same day over until he finally gets it right. But getting it right will involves countless mistakes and misguided efforts, and, furthermore, it will require some fundamental changes in who Phil is. The self-centered Phil must be replaced by a new Phil who is able to love others and care about their well-being. Only when the new Phil is born will his day of triumph be possible.

From the perspective of the viewer of the film, it is obvious that the self-centered early Phil is not a happy person. While his sole concern is his own gratification, his obvious lack of interest in anything beyond himself limits his ability to find much gratification. He devotes himself to satisfying various impulses, but none of these satisfactions add up to a satisfying life. At one point Rita says to Phil in frustration, "You'll never love anyone but yourself." Phil responds spontaneously, "That's not true. I don't even like myself."

Phil's failure to like himself is not surprising. There is not much to like about his narrow and constricted self. When he is given an unlimited opportunity to seek gratifications for that self, he pursues a variety of manipulative schemes, none of which yield any lasting satisfaction. He can have what he wants, but getting what he wants results in boredom, disappointment and eventually despair. It might have taken a lifetime for Phil to discover the emptiness of his pursuits. But the opportunity to try them all out with the aid of godlike knowledge reveals to Phil that no matter how much he gets, he will still be stuck with a self he does not like and gratifications that fade quickly.

When Phil begins to pursue Rita, it is with the same manipulative mentality that had characterized his previous pursuits. She is simply another conquest. However, he realizes that to achieve his aims, he must appear to be something different from what he is. So Phil begins to play the part of a different person. He is attentive and gentle and kind because that is the sort of man Rita will respond to. While Phil is able to play this part convincingly, he is not able to pull it off completely. Repeatedly, at a crucial point, the manipulative Phil appears and Rita is repulsed.

When Phil realizes that the things he can have won't satisfy him and that what might bring him satisfaction is beyond his grasp, he is plunged into despair. With the option of suicide denied him, Phil reaches out to Rita for help. This time, however, he approaches her, not with the same ulterior motives, but with a kind of desperate need. No longer viewing Rita as an object to manipulate, Phil begins to admire her kindness and compassion. It is Rita who suggests to him that what is happening may not be a curse. As she puts it, "It depends on how you look at it."

Phil begins to look on his plight as an opportunity to change his whole approach to life. Instead of viewing each event in terms of personal gain, he starts to look for ways of helping others. Eventually these activities result in an ability to care about others and to get satisfaction from benefitting them. As Phil is learning to care about other people, he is also learning to care about himself. He becomes interested in exploring literature and in developing his creative talents. Instead of seeking merely to satisfy himself, he is working to build a self.

The contrast between the early Phil and the later Phil is remarkable. The early Phil lives in a self-imposed prison which closes him off to a fuller life. The later Phil has become a person with a range of interests beyond his own life. He has become an expanded self who is able to experience satisfactions that were previously unavailable to him. Furthermore, he has come to enjoy being the person he is.

THE PROSPECT OF EXPANSION

Self-centeredness comes in degrees. The early Phil is an extreme case, virtually devoid of concerns for anyone around him and completely enamored with his own aggrandizement. From an external viewpoint his life appears as a kind of trap. Fulfilling his urges toward personal gratification would be unlikely to produce much happiness, yet the possibility of finding a more satisfying life is blocked by the limitations he has imposed on himself. As long as others are only objects to use in furthering his aims, the satisfactions that come from love and friendship are like a closed book to him.

To live a fuller life, Phil needs to develop concerns for things beyond himself. He must learn to value other people, not merely as means to achieve his own advancement, but because he recognizes in them some worth independent of their usefulness. He needs to learn to care about values such as beauty and truth that transcend his personal aims. In short, he needs to have some interests that lift him out of the narrow circle of concerns that hold him captive.

Attempting to fulfill the interests of his current self may yield much gratification, but the life he can hope for is severely limited in comparison with the kind of life he might achieve if he had a different self, a self with a wider range of concerns. Paradoxically, the way to care for his self is not by giving that self what it wants, but by replacing that self. Only when he has built into the self a fundamentally different set of concerns will he discover the route to a more satisfying life.

From an observer's perspective it is apparent that Phil's transformation improves his life. Imagine, however, that someone had tried to reason with the early Phil to convince him that he needed to change. From his cynical and self-serving point of view it would have been difficult to see why such a change should be sought. In fact it seems likely that the early Phil would have viewed a life in which concern for others played an important part to be either a pretense or a misguided confusion. If someone had tried to explain to him the satisfactions available from such a life, he would have found the explanation virtually incomprehensible, for translated into his way of understanding life, the alternative makes little sense.

From the early Phil's point of view relationships are useful for various purposes, but genuinely caring about another person is not particularly useful. It may be valuable to appear to care. Phil could acknowledge that he is more likely to get what he wants from others if they assume he values them or think he is their friend. But from his viewpoint these appearances are all strategic maneuvers designed to enable him to use others.

From such a perspective, actually coming to care about another person would be a distraction from efficiently pursuing his own advancement. It might lead him to use his energies to help someone who is unable to benefit him in return, or even worse, he might suffer grief at the misfortune of someone he cared about. To avoid conflicts with the diligent pursuit of his own interest, he must avoid any real attachments to others that might dilute his devotion to his personal interests. In other words, he must make sure that he does not become an expanded self.

Avoiding real attachments need not mean, of course, that Phil gives up the quest for benefits he can get from others. If certain benefits depend on appearing to care about others, he can do his best to play the role of a caring person. In fact, a Phil who reflected on how to effectively pursue his interest would be unlikely very often to display himself as the obnoxious self-absorbed jerk he appears at the beginning of the film. To get what he wants from others, he will most of the time want to cultivate the image of a kind and considerate person. Perfecting such a role would require considerable effort. It is not enough to get the lines right; he must avoid any nonverbal messages or inflections that might give away his true intentions. Perhaps he can drop the act occasionally, but he needs to be able to put the mask on at a moment's notice.

There is some question about whether many people could actually give a successful performance of caring for others while remaining free of any actual attachments. One reason is that in close relationships (in contrast with casual or superficial relationships) just going through the motions eventually shows itself for what it is. The wife whose husband engages in most of the correct behaviors may still detect that when the choice is between his well-being and hers, her interests never really weigh heavily. She is likely to realize that his presentation of himself as a loving husband does not fit well with what is revealed in moments when he is not fully guarded. It is difficult to fool those with whom we have extended and close interactions.

One way to deal with this problem is to dispense with close relationships, keeping things on a superficial level. An alternative is to rely on one's personal powers of persuasion and charm to keep the other person from regarding slips of the mask as significant. Such a strategy might give one considerable time, during which the other person would be likely to develop an attachment strong enough to obscure insights into the real nature of the relationship.

Even so, a person who set out to live a life of pretense, able to put in a credible imitation of a caring person would face another difficulty. Human beings tend to actually form attachments to others, and acting as if you care about someone is a way of actually coming to care about the other person. It would be a rare individual who could expect to avoid attachments entirely, though it is possible to minimize actual caring and make manipulative interactions the predominant style.

The question, for each of us, however, is not merely whether such a lifestyle is possible. It is whether we could choose to become the kind of self capable of living that sort of life. When we think reflectively about our own lives, it seems unlikely that many of us would choose to become a self with literally no concern for anyone else. Such a person would be scarcely recognizable to us as human. We know that there are mothers with no concern for their children, husbands who have no concern for their wives, and people who have no relationships other than those founded on business needs. But these ways of living are often not reflective choices; they are typically a product of some severe incapacity or a poverty of imagination about the possibilities for relationship or they are a lifestyle that one has drifted into mindlessly.

Most of us find ourselves already caring about some others:

parents, brothers and sisters, friends, romantic attachments, even strangers. Imagine passing a child who is trapped in an automobile that has caught fire. While many people have their limits on what they will do to help, it would be a very unusual person who literally had no concern about whether the child escaped. How deep our attachments and our concerns for others go depends on a variety of factors, but few of us would consciously choose to eliminate the caring connections we already have.

What we might consider is whether to become more caring. Should I cultivate deeper friendships? Should I become more interested in the lives of the employees I manage? Should I become less manipulative in my romantic relationships? Should I take an interest in the problem of starvation in underdeveloped countries? By reflecting on the depth of our concerns and the extent of our caring, we open ourselves to the possibility of change. When we reflect seriously on these matters, we are thinking, not just about modifications in behavior, but modifications in the set of concerns that help to define who we are.

SELF-INTEREST AND CARING

Even if the early Phil would be difficult to convince, most of us can see how the presence of friendships and love relationships can improve our lives. The self that can expand to genuinely care about other people and to form caring attachments is more likely than the isolated self to live the kind of life that we could be satisfied with. Hence, building into ourselves the capacities for developing caring relationships and cultivating opportunities conducive to forming a few connections of this sort has a strong appeal. If we think in this way, are we in effect making a self-interested choice to become interested in something beyond the self?

Putting the matter in that way is misleading. Thinking of the choice as self-interested suggests that when we weigh potential benefits of each way of living, the caring life will yield greater benefits. However, when we try to compare the benefits of these different ways of living, we have no common scale of measurement to make a comparison, since the benefits valued by a caring self will not be the same as the benefits valued by an uncaring self. The superiority of one life to the other is not to be decided by self-interested thinking, for to apply such thinking we need to have already settled on a self that supplies a standard for measuring interests.

It might be thought that we could measure and compare the satisfaction levels of various alternative selves. However, even if there was a way to do this, it would be unwise to assume that the self achieving the greatest amount of satisfaction or the greatest balance of satisfaction over dissatisfaction lived the kind of life that is most desirable. It is entirely possible that the life with the highest balance of satisfaction over dissatisfaction would belong to someone who had very limited capacities for the kinds of satisfaction which carry with them the possibility for disappointment. Yet if we understood what those satisfactions involved, we might judge a life containing them to be worth more than a life without them. In fact, a life containing the risk of major disappointments might be judged preferable to a life which guarded against disappointments. ("Tis better to have loved and lost than never to have loved at all."[4])

Our judgment that a life exercising the capacity for caring relationships is better than a life which does not, rests not so much on counting and comparing satisfactions as it does on applying an ideal of human living which incorporates what we judge to be valuable or important. If we call the caring kind of life a happier life, we are using the term "happiness" not just to describe some aspect of the life, but to endorse that way of living.[5] The fact that the early Phil is clearly dissatisfied and that we can predict that most people taking his approach to life will be dissatisfied, makes it easier to judge his life unhappy. But even if Phil were completely satisfied with his life, most of us would have difficulty giving such a life our endorsement, for it fails to measure up to our conception of happiness.

In making such a judgment, however, we are taking the perspective of one who recognizes the value of caring relationships as an important element in a worthwhile life. From that perspective, a life without caring relationships seems not only isolated, but lacking in the kind of satisfaction crucial to the life we could aspire to live. Even if we were convinced that with some kind of indoctrination program we could eventually get used to and be satisfied with such a life, we would judge it from our present perspective to be empty, lacking in significance, or shallow. The kind of satisfaction that is crucial is that which can incorporate our deepest reflective values.

When we think about choosing a self, we are attempting to discover what type of self could be for us an object of admiration or at least respect. As we reflect on our values, we are trying to articulate what we would need to be to live the kind of life we could judge worthwhile. Once we have chosen a self, we can raise the self-interested question of how to benefit that self, but the choice provides the standard needed for weighing potential benefits and harms. Hence, the choice of a self is not a self-interested choice, but a prerequisite to being able to make clear judgments of self-interest.

Even if the choice of becoming a caring self were construed to be a self-interested choice, it would be the kind of choice which should be distinguished from most self-interested choices. Deciding to incorporate concerns for other people is a choice to be motivated by something other than self-interest. The person who acts on this decision will internalize habits of thinking and feeling which are in conflict with a purely egoistic approach to each situation. One who has developed such habits cannot simply turn them on or off at will, for genuine concerns will become a part of a relatively stable psychological structure. They cannot coexist with the kind of calculating rationality which evaluates each act in terms of personal benefit, for the person who cares about others is concerned with things other than personal benefit.

THE ENJOYMENTS OF CARING RELATIONSHIPS

People who care about others generally get some enjoyment from being with and pleasing those they care about. This fact leads some to suspect that altruistic behaviors can be motivated by self-interest. There is a truth in this suspicion, but the truth is easily misunderstood. The truth is that for the self which has expanded to include concerns for the well-being of others, the lines between self-interested action and altruistic action are not as sharp as they would be for an unexpanded self. If Foster loves Caroline, he may go to great lengths to find an exactly appropriate present for her birthday. Since he cares about her, he will naturally get some enjoyment from doing something that gives her pleasure. If we ask, "Did he do it for himself?" there is an unproblematic sense in which we can say yes. The self which has incorporated a concern for Caroline benefits from benefitting her.

However, the claim that he did it for himself may be misleading, if we understand doing something for oneself to be contrasted with doing it for another. Someone who imagines that Foster is motivated only by his own enjoyment is unlikely to understand his action, for the enjoyment in question is one that depends on caring about someone else. If he did not care about Caroline, Foster would not be so gratified at pleasing her. He is able to get enjoyment precisely because of the value he puts on something distinct from his own enjoyment.

Imagine a different person, Pamela, who has not incorporated into herself a concern for Ted, but seeks to get the benefits of a relationship with Ted. Pamela might desire to do some things which will please Ted in order to get him to do things that she wants, but if we imagine that Pamela does not care about Ted, pleasing him should not in itself be a source of gratification. It will only be a means to an independent end. Whatever benefits Pamela may get from her relationship, the joys that could come from loving Ted or caring about his welfare will not be a part of her experience. Of course, it is possible for Pamela to regard any enjoyments that depend on actually caring about someone else as unimportant, but if so, her assessment would differ significantly from most people's.

Most of us think of the enjoyments of friendship or love as crucial elements in a desirable life. Few would be willing to trade the joys that come from caring relationships for a life that was filled with other kinds of pleasure, but lacked deep human attachments.[6] We find in such relationships a type of fulfillment that seems vital to living a full life. Hence, expanding the self to include concerns for others is for most people an entirely reasonable choice.

While expanding the self to care about others opens up the possibility of a range of satisfactions, it is not without its risks. Caring about others makes us vulnerable to a range of disappointments and frustrations as well. The child you adore may break your heart by throwing his life away on tempting frivolities. The friend you counted on may prove unreliable when you need her most. The spouse you gave yourself to unreservedly may come to regard your love with contempt. There is only one way to protect yourself from these eventualities. It is by refusing to care. When we care deeply for another person, the price we pay for loss or betrayal or indifference can be overwhelming. Yet while we should be careful before committing ourselves unreservedly, a life of holding back from others has its own drawbacks. Some risks we may judge worth taking.

It is important to recognize that some of the risks involved in caring for others result from the fact that genuine caring runs deep within a person. We cannot both care and keep our options entirely open with regard to another. While there may be degrees of caring, the degree to which we do care is not something that we can turn on or off at will. If we try to maintain the sort of detachment toward others that would enable us to withdraw our affections at the first sign that we were losing more than we were gaining from the relationship, we are adopting a stance that effectively closes us off from the most important benefits of caring relationships.

SELF AND OTHERS

Sometimes people make a sharp distinction between benefitting yourself and benefitting others, thinking that actions of one kind are typically in conflict with actions of the other kind. However, in many cases helping others can be done with little or no sacrifice to personal interests, and for the self that has incorporated concerns for others, advancement of the interests of the person cared about can be regarded as advancement for the self as well. When the child I care about does well, my own interests are served in addition to the child's interests.

Nevertheless, there can be conflicts between doing what is good for others and doing what is good for yourself, even for an expanded self. Just as an individual who lacks concern for others can still experience a tension among competing impulses, the expanded self is likely to find a tension in bringing together various disparate aims. Some other-directed ends will be likely to conflict with more purely personal aims. For example, suppose Diane, a single parent, cares greatly about her son, wanting to provide him with the best education possible. Achieving this aim may be difficult to reconcile with the demands of a limited budget. Her contribution to her son's education may be a benefit to her as well, but it is in competition with a range of other desires, including some nonaltruistic ones.

Imagine a situation where Diane cares enough about her son to give up a hearing aid she needs. Diane can get along without the hearing aid, but the quality of her life and the effectiveness of her work would be improved with one. Even though Diane is an expanded self, it is implausible to call her action self-interested. More generally, when a person with altruistic desires, allows those desires to determine action and those desires conflict significantly with personal needs, the act exemplifies self-sacrifice rather than self-interest.[7] The fact that benefitting someone you care about may sometimes be both altruistic and self-interested does not show that it always is.

When we recognize that the self which expands to incorporate concern for others is faced with potential tension between other-directed aims and more purely personal aims, we may suspect that one could become an overexpanded or an overextended self. Since individual human beings have finite resources of time and energy, there is some danger of developing relationships which require more than can reasonably be given. There is some reason to think that this is a danger that women are more susceptible to than men. For whatever reason, men tend to be more guarded in their commitments to others and more protective of their personal space. The typical male problem is having too few close personal relationships or having relationships that are fairly superficial and undemanding. On the other hand women are drawn by genetics or socialization to connections that require considerable time and effort.

For some women the danger is that concern for others will squeeze out the kind of concern that should be directed toward their own needs. By training or inclination a woman may become so caught up in the needs of family and friends that she virtually loses herself.[8] Taking the expanded self as an ideal need not mean adopting altruistic aims to the extent that they overwhelm any other kinds of aims. In fact, such a possibility scarcely seems consistent with maintaining a proper degree of self-respect. An individual who regards her own needs as important may find it necessary to acquire some balance which enables her to maintain a self that is recognized as valuable in its own right, and not just as useful to others. Maintaining such a self does not have to rule out the possibility of self-sacrifice, but a self which is all sacrifice has lost something vital.

Caring deeply about others does not have to mean neglecting your own needs and development. However, just as judgment is necessary to decide what personal interests to pursue, it is necessary in deciding what can be given to others and what is beyond the resources you are able to invest. Although this sounds like an attempt to ration love, it might be more accurately described as maintaining the kind of self that has something of importance to give. For the most valuable gifts are those we can offer in a context of mutual respect and freedom. Furthermore, the kind of giving that leaves us perpetually unsatisfied is difficult to sustain indefinitely.

In addition to the question of how much we can offer those in relatively close relationships, each of us faces the question of how far to extend the circle of our concerns. In *Groundhog Day* Phil's expanded self has come to care in the end about the whole community, lending his aid to virtually anyone in need. This sort of attitude is at least imaginable in a small-town setting; it becomes more difficult to understand how it could work in an urban setting where anonymity and indifference to strangers seem necessary as a survival technique. We simply cannot offer to everyone the kind of caring and attention we offer to those in the necessarily narrow circle of intimate friends.

When religious traditions tell us to love our neighbor as ourself and then tell us that every person is to be regarded as our neighbor, the demand appears to be greater than we can deliver. In order not to be driven wild by the ideal, a person committed to such a tradition would need to temper its demands by understanding what is owed to the distant neighbor as somewhat less than what is owed to those in the network of close relationships and commitments. Nevertheless, such ideals remind us of an important truth: that people in the particular circle of relationships in which we have considerable emotional and material connections are, from a larger point of view, no more important than people on the other side of the world we will never meet or understand. Even if we cannot feel toward the stranger the same kind of warmhearted caring that we have for intimate friends, we can understand that this person has a claim to worth as significant as the claims of those we love.

When we think about our lives from a less biased and more impartial point of view, it is difficult to think that the people we care about are valuable without extending our recognition of value to the stranger as well. While it is unrealistic and impractical to say that we will do for the stranger what we will do for the friend, regarding the stranger with complete indifference is difficult for a reflective person to square psychologically with the empathetic capacities needed for close relationships. Furthermore, when we reflect on the ideal self of our aspirations, few of us are entirely pleased at the prospect of being a self who is untouched by the sufferings of the world and unwilling to lift a finger to help those in desperate need.[9]

There are costs in becoming an expanded self who has developed the capacity to empathize with others and who is concerned with their needs. Becoming such a self probably increases one's chance for severe disappointment and frustration. But the alternative to becoming such a self has its own drawbacks. In the end each of us needs to decide whether we are content to live an existence focused only on our own needs. In varying degrees we have the option of allowing the needs of others to be an important influence on our thoughts, emotions, and actions. Our willingness to incorporate into the self concerns for the well-being of others is crucial to determining what way of life will be possible for us, and the option of changing the self in this direction is not open to us indefinitely. Unlike Phil we do not have infinite time to alter our course until we get it right.

Chapter Six

THE LIMITED SELF

...can it profit a man to take money unjustly, if he is thereby enslaving the best part of his nature to the vilest? (Socrates in Plato's *Republic*[1])

...a truly successful strategy of deception effectively cuts oneself off from the community in which alone one can find the confirmation essential to one's sense of self. (Gerald Postema[2])

...the truly ethical person has an inner serenity and sense of security, for he does not have duty outside himself but within himself. (Judge Wilhelm in Kierkegaard's *Either/Or*[3])

Woody Allen's film, *Crimes and Misdemeanors*[4], confronts us with a central question for anyone who reflects seriously about what kind of life to live: Can you get away with murder? Or more generally, do you have good reason to observe moral restrictions even when you can profitably violate them without getting caught?

Judah, the story's central character, is a wealthy and respected ophthalmologist who, as the film opens, is accepting an award at a banquet for his leadership in a philanthropic campaign to establish a new hospital wing. His public persona is in tension, however, with the life Judah has been living. While appearing to be a loving and committed husband and father, he has for years been having an affair with Delores, who now insists that Judah leave his wife. When Judah refuses, Delores threatens to reveal not only the affair, but also certain financial irregularities regarding Judah's handling of charitable funds, which he has managed to cover up. With his well-ordered life about to unravel, Judah is desperate to find some solution.

When buying his mistress off proves fruitless, Judah seeks advice from his longtime friend and patient, Rabbi Ben. Ben tells Judah that his only alternative is to confess the affair to his wife and hope for her forgiveness. Unwilling to take this approach, Judah seeks out his brother, Jack, who has underworld connections. Jack offers to solve the problem by arranging for a hit man to kill the mistress. At first Judah categorically rejects this idea, but as Delores becomes increasingly insistent on disrupting his stable life, he tells his brother to proceed with the plan.

After the murder Judah is emotionally undone. Though he is not a religious man, his religious upbringing returns in his imagination with a powerful force. He remembers the words of his father that the eyes of God see all and that God will reward the righteous and punish the wicked. Hardly able to function, Judah becomes anxious and distracted. He is so overcome by guilt that he begins to seriously consider going to the police and confessing.

Meanwhile the police have discovered that Delores had phoned Judah at his office and at home. When a detective checks this out, Judah is able to claim convincingly that she was an overanxious patient. He feels sure that the police must suspect something, but in fact they are satisfied, and Judah is left to struggle with his conscience.

Months pass, and in a pivotal scene we see Judah at a party talking to a producer of film documentaries. Judah tells him of an idea for a murder story with a strange twist. A highly successful man commits a murder to protect what he has.

> ... and after the awful deed is done he finds that he's plagued by deep-rooted guilt. Little sparks of his religious background which he'd rejected are suddenly stirred up. He hears his father's voice. He imagines that God is watching every move. Suddenly it's not an empty universe at all, but a just and moral one, and he's violated it. Now he's panic stricken. He's on the verge of a mental collapse, an inch away from confessing the whole thing to the police, and then one morning he awakens. The sun is shining and his family is around him and mysteriously the crisis is lifted. He takes his family on a vacation to Europe, and as the

> months pass, he finds that he's not punished. In fact he prospers. The killing gets attributed to another person, a drifter who has a number of other murders.... Now he's scot-free. His life is completely back to normal—back to his protected world of wealth and privilege. Once in a while he has a bad moment, but in time it passes.[5]

According to Judah's autobiographical account, he has gotten away with murder. Not only has he escaped detection by the police; he has battled his own conscience and emerged victorious. When Judah was in deepest despair, he feared that the teaching of his childhood was true—that we live in a moral universe where the wicked will suffer and the righteous will prosper. But he now finds this view belied by his own experience. He has violated the precepts of morality, and after going through a rough period, he has emerged with his career and family intact, ready to resume a life of privilege and prosperity.

MORALITY AND SELF-INTEREST

Judah's story goes against the grain of our preferred way of thinking about the world. We like those stories in which the guilty are caught and given an appropriate punishment. We enjoy tales in which deserving people get their due reward. But stories of unjust suffering by good people or undeserved prosperity by bad people leave us with a strong sense of discomfort.

In the film the conflict between two opposing views of life is dramatically portrayed in a half-remembered, half-imagined argument at the family dinner table of Judah's childhood. Judah's sister argues that might makes right. Those who are powerful enough to flout moral conventions in the pursuit of what they want need not be bound by anyone else's rules. Those who want to live in accordance with moral restrictions can do so, but some people make their own rules. Judah's father argues that there is a moral structure to the universe. Those who violate this structure will face the consequences. A person who commits a crime will be punished "in one way or another." Judah's sister claims, "If he can do it and get away with it, and he chooses not to be bothered by the ethics, then he's home free." Judah's experience appears to confirm his sister's side of the argument.

According to that side, there is no moral structure to the universe that guarantees to fit the punishment to the crime. There are, of course, various human punishments and social sanctions which a prudent person will want to take into account. But when the chances of being caught are low and the benefits of risking the penalties are great enough, society's threats may not provide compelling reason to accept the restrictions of morality. Sometimes a person has a pretty good chance of maintaining a respectable reputation and the benefits it provides, while bending or breaking the rules. Without the kind of moral structure that gives the rules real clout, why should such a person sacrifice personal gain to obey the rules?

One who accepts this view need not think it advisable to break every rule in sight. There are advantages in appearing to be a person of high moral standards, and usually the best way to create such an appearance is by observing the rules most of the time. Furthermore, it would be undesirable to put yourself in a position requiring constant worry about the possibility of detection. But when the potential benefits are high enough and the risks small enough, someone who doubts the existence of a moral structure might find the risks worth taking.

Many people, including Rabbi Ben in the film, find the denial of a moral structure to the universe intolerable. Though they admit that the wicked may appear to prosper and the righteous may appear to suffer, they are convinced that underneath the appearances is a reality in which evil is ultimately punished and good is ultimately rewarded. Sometimes this conviction is grounded in religious beliefs appealing to God's righteous judgment or an impersonal law of karma which guarantees justice in a subsequent life. However, even people who lack any religious basis for expecting moral living to pay off can be reluctant to give up belief in a moral order which connects obeying the rules with an individual's self-interest.

Consider the ways people talk about their reasons for observing moral standards: "I treat others fairly," announced a businessman, "so I can sleep at night." Moral training often reflects a similar orientation, as, for example, when young people are told to avoid lies because "the truth is easier to remember." The tendency to assume that there is a self-interested basis for moral behavior probably accounts for the popularity of such slogans as, "Honesty is the best policy," or "What goes around, comes around." These slogans draw our attention to potential payoffs of moral living and potential risks of immorality. They give expression to a kind of faith that moral behavior coincides with doing what benefits you most, at least in the long term.

If we confine ourselves to empirical observation, this sort of faith appears to outrun the evidence. Without question, it is usually in a person's interest to abide by most moral restrictions. Most of the time it pays to keep your promises and pay your debts and refrain from harming others. But sometimes a well-told lie can get you out of a tight spot, or you can take advantage of a stranger without much worry about negative ramifications, or you can weasel out of a commitment that demands more than you are willing to give. More dramatically, there can be times when crime pays off handsomely and criminals go scot-free. Judah's story may not portray what always or typically happens to those who violate the rules, but ordinary observation suggests that some people who violate the rules do quite well. Whether or not justice is assured in an afterlife, it is not always accomplished in this life.

SELF-INTEREST AND CONSCIENCE

Those who think that there is always a self-interested reason to observe the rules sometimes appeal to conscience as an enforcer of morality. Even if you are not detected by society or if societal sanctions are too weak to be an effective deterrent, you must live with your own conscience, and the punishments of conscience can be quite severe. Perhaps this is what Judah's father had in mind when he said that one who violates the moral law will be punished "in one way or another."

However, the problem with thinking that conscience always gives one a self-interested reason for moral behavior is twofold:

First, many people have remarkably weak consciences and enormous capacities for rationalization and self-deception. The employee who steals from the boss is often fully convinced that what is taken is owed in some way. The woman who becomes involved with a married man comforts herself with the thought that the wife has not treated the husband well and does not deserve to keep him. The salesperson who lies about a product is convinced that "this is the way the game is played." Even if we imagine people who have been well brought up and clearly know how to judge the difference between right and wrong, there is considerable distortion in the way people think about their own deeds. It is surprisingly rare to find an individual who judges himself with the same kind of rigor and objectivity that he exercises with others.

Related to the issue of how effectively conscience is working is the fact that we ultimately have control over how much our conscience will bother us. Suppose that Helen does something which is clearly wrong by her own standards and that she begins to feel guilty and despondent. Helen has a number of options. One is to take the view that there is no use "crying over spilt milk" and to take steps to get over her bad feelings. She might accomplish this goal by adjusting her standards to make them easier to fulfill or by making allowances for herself or by redescribing her actions in more flattering terms. If she finds her guilt feelings troubling enough, she might even try to reprogram her conscience so that she no longer reacts in the same way.

Just as a surgeon might desensitize herself to be able to cut on a human body without squeamishness, a person with a troublesome conscience can desensitize herself to guilt feelings in some area. Perhaps the easiest way to do this is simply by continuing to engage in the activity. The first time you cheat on your taxes, you may experience a high level of anxiety. But the more you do it, the less you think about it, eventually coming to the point where it scarcely bothers you at all. The same sort of process can alter our inhibitions even to such acts as murder. The professional killer may have initially felt some human queasiness, but his natural human reactions are likely to recede as killing becomes more routine.

Having a strong conscience requires both development through proper training and maintenance through engaging in the thoughts and actions conducive to keeping moral sensitivities functioning. A willingness to "go with the flow" can easily alter one's conscience to the point where it is flexible enough not to interfere with strong inclinations. There may be limits to our ability to reprogram our consciences, but a concerted effort can often diminish or extinguish guilt feelings we don't want to be bothered with.

Hence, for the person who chooses not to internalize particular moral restrictions, the warning that conscience will intervene to punish the evildoer need not carry great weight. The people who are bothered most by conscience are those who have done what it takes to maintain their moral sensitivities. Those who have allowed their conscience to atrophy or distanced themselves from moral principles may celebrate their freedom from the limitations that conscience imposes.

Ultimately the question of whether conscience provides a self-interested reason for abiding by moral restrictions depends on what kind of self a person chooses to become. If I seek to be the kind of self who is unlimited by moral principles, I can declare my independence, at least to some extent, from the harsh rule of conscience. If, however, I aspire to be a self whose behavior is governed by moral principles, then conscience can play a vital role in living that life. Choosing to become a moral self means choosing to make certain limitations a part of you, and having such internal constraints makes it easier to sustain moral behavior patterns.

What seems puzzling is why anyone would want to become a self with internalized limits on the pursuit of his or her goals. It is one thing to avoid lying because you might get caught or because you might feel bad. However, these motivations are distinguishable from avoiding lies because you have chosen to build into yourself a restriction on telling lies. To some people the idea of building in such a restriction sounds a little like tying your ankles together before the start of a race.

LIMITATION BY PRINCIPLE

Why might I want to be the kind of self who feels bad as a result of harming another person? One reason is that a lack of feelings would indicate a lack of concern for the other person. In the last chapter I suggested that there are reasons to become the kind of self who has at least some caring connections with others. People who recognize the importance of expanding the self to include caring connections ought to understand the value of internal restraints of some kind with regard to those they care about. If you can harm someone you claim to care about without regret, that is a sign that you lack any real concern for the person. Furthermore, genuine caring requires a developed capacity for putting yourself in the other person's place. The ability to understand another person empathetically is crucial to intelligently acting for the other's benefit. But empathetic reactions cannot be maintained by a person who is able to disregard the other person's interest without any qualms. When I lie to, steal from, or cheat another person, I need to be able to suppress the kinds of feelings that an empathetic understanding would evoke, for responding to another with empathy makes me vividly aware of the importance of that person's interests.

Suppose someone says, "I can understand why I might want to be the kind of person who feels bad at the misfortune of those I love or care about, particularly about the misfortune that I inflict. But why would I want to have internalized inhibitions toward harming people I do not care about at all?

To answer this question, we need to understand fully what is being proposed. The possibility suggested is to build into the self some principles of restraint, but limit the scope of these principles to certain individuals. The strategy is to exercise internal restraint with regard to cheating your friends or relatives, but have no qualms about cheating strangers or mere acquaintances when you can get away with it. Such a strategy sounds like a description of the way some people try to live. The idea is to be a moral self in relation to some people and an amoral self in relation to others.

One question about this strategy is how psychologically viable it is. To attempt to regard some people as objects for manipulation requires a degree of desensitization to those people. It means suppressing any human feelings and habitually allowing calculative ways of thinking about personal advantage to govern any interactions. But if I have learned how to relate to others as if I were playing some kind of competitive game, can I expect to turn off this mode and become a loving self with my family and friends? Isn't it likely that the manipulative way of thinking and behaving will seep over into the area of my life I had hoped to preserve for caring relationships? The problem with becoming skilled at disregarding the interests of others is that the habits necessary for disregard are difficult to put on or take off at will. Hence, radically limiting the scope of internalized principles threatens to weaken our capacity for caring relationships.

Of course, the capacities at issue are matters of degree, and perhaps someone might think it possible to treat those outside the favored circle with a degree of decency while maintaining a sufficient capacity to love. However, it is difficult to know in advance whether the kind of balance you are trying to strike will be sustainable, for essentially the strategy is to maintain within a single life alternate selves who are in tension with each other.

Another problem with trying to limit the scope of moral principles is that it introduces a kind of arbitrariness which is intellectually unsatisfying. The people whose interests we are willing to ignore are not all that different from the people on whom we bestow our care and concern. The fact that one group of people falls within your circle of friends and another does not may furnish some basis for differential treatment. But it cannot be that the interests of your friends matter only because they happen to be your friends. The kind of moral sensibility which enables me to form an imaginative appreciation of why the needs of my friends matter is difficult to isolate from my capacity for moving beyond my personal perspective to a more objective point of view. Yet my understanding that what is worth caring about in my friends is worth caring about in others threatens to break down a sharp division between my own circle of concern and people who fall outside that circle. The reflective person who cares about some people is pushed toward recognizing that those who are not cared about directly may, nevertheless, deserve some degree of respect.[6]

PUBLIC AND PRIVATE SELF-IMAGES

One day in my business ethics class I described for students a scenario in which a businessperson has an opportunity for significant personal profit by breaking an ethical rule. "What would be the right thing to do in this situation?" I asked the class. Students had little difficulty imagining themselves in the situation the businessperson faced, and as they identified with the businessperson, several offered relatively weak attempts to justify the very tempting behavior. Finally one student came to the end of his patience with these rationalizations. "Of course, it's wrong," he said, "but I would do it."

This student was not claiming that questions of right or wrong are always irrelevant in deciding what to do. Rather he was saying that when it comes down to a choice between doing what is right and getting some significant personal benefit, it would be more important to him to gain the benefit. What is striking about this student's remark is the fact that he stated his willingness so publicly. There are many people who would behave in the way he endorses, but few people are willing to announce that under certain circumstances they will ignore the rules for the sake of personal gain. If someone does exhibit a public intention not to be bound by ethical rules, the most natural way for other people to respond is by withdrawing their trust from this person.

Responding to others with trust is a part of ordinary living. Often we let down the guard to some degree, refraining from protecting ourselves from the various ways others might do us damage. If we could never let down our guard, we would spend so much time and energy on self-protection that we could accomplish little else. Relying on other people not to sell contaminated food or to stay on their own side of the road, or to keep their commitments is often a reasonable and productive way to behave, but what makes such behavior reasonable is a functioning moral code which people generally observe. No code will be one-hundred percent effective in preventing undesirable behavior; some people will opt out of the rules and others will observe them selectively. However, when a moral code is functioning well enough to give a relative security against certain risks, it can often be reasonable to exhibit appropriate degrees of trust.

Gaining the trust of others is often necessary for effectively pursuing some goals. The person who wants to sell you a product or get your cooperation in a joint project or start a romantic relationship with you needs to have your trust and must, therefore, portray herself as trustworthy. In general, getting what we want from others requires us to use their trust, and that trust is given on the assumption that we are willing to limit the pursuit of our self-interest in accordance with understood rules.

The practical necessity of portraying ourselves as trustworthy reveals why my student's announced willingness to disregard the rules seems odd. The announcement seems to work against his own interest in maintaining a reputation for trustworthiness. The person who is willing to lie, cheat, or steal usually does not want others to be aware of that willingness. Otherwise they will protect themselves in ways that make it difficult to achieve the aims that lying, stealing, and cheating are used to accomplish.

The need to maintain a public reputation for trustworthiness means that the person who is unwilling to be limited by moral constraints must develop a public image which differs from the private reality. If I am willing to be sneaky and underhanded, I will not want others to perceive me as such. I will want to convey the appearance in observable behavior and self-descriptions of someone who is honest and reliable and concerned for the well-being of others. The image I have of myself in such a case should be different from the image I present for public consumption.

Of course, everyone's public and private images probably differ to some degree, but the self without moral limits would be miles away from anything that could be portrayed openly. The distance between these two images gives rise to several kinds of pressure. One is the pressure to maintain the proper public image. Considerable calculation of the effects of various ways of behaving is called for. What can I keep secret? What are the odds of detection? Which people have sufficient power to damage my reputation? How will a particular way of portraying myself come across to others? The life devoted to maintaining a public persona which is in tension with one's private identity can be quite demanding.

Another kind of pressure arises from the difficulty of acknowledging your own nature to yourself. The things we hide from others because we expect their condemnation are typically not easy to face up to in ourselves. Rather than viewing myself as dishonest, I will think of myself as one who occasionally cuts corners in minor ways. Rather than admitting that I am involved in an adulterous relationship, I will think about how I am breaking out of an overly confining marriage. It is difficult to separate the power to judge ourselves from the public judgments we share with others, and, hence, we typically cope with a major divergence by means of self-deception. Refraining from internalizing communal norms usually means becoming a self that you cannot be proud of and must use self-deception to avoid acknowledging.

When Judah in *Crimes and Misdemeanors* comes to the point where he is able to live with his choice of murder, he is able to think that he has made it "scot-free." However, the freedom from the harsh judgment of conscience he has been able to achieve is not without cost. If Judah is like most of us, his self-esteem depends, not just on his private appraisal of his merits, but the public appraisal of others. However, in violating the standards that Judah himself affirms publicly, he can maintain a high estimation of his own worth only by massive self-deception and suppression or by attempting to substitute private appraisals which diverge significantly from public ones.

Developing private standards to judge your own worth is much more difficult than it might seem. A murderer may be able to admire the cleverness and daring with which her plan is executed. She might admire the skill with which she conned others into aiding with the plan. But this approach is essentially a matter of "borrowing" aspects of a system of public appraisal and leaving off other aspects. However, it is problematic to borrow only those aspects of the public system which will allow us to affirm ourselves and to leave off aspects which would condemn us. Those parts that we leave off are often integrally connected with the parts we would like to adopt.

If Judah acknowledges to himself that he is the kind of person willing to kill another person to protect his reputation and social standing, he cannot seriously think of himself as a decent, law-abiding citizen or as a person who lives by the golden rule. Many of the ideals which might have been used to bolster his own sense of worth will have to drop off. The most likely way for him to develop a conscience which no longer bothers him is to cease or greatly diminish any reflection on what he is. Facing up to the truth about himself means giving up many of the images by which he could have viewed his worth in terms of his place as a member of a larger community.

From the point of view of someone who is considering what kind of self to become, the issue is not whether someone like Judah might make peace with himself and become fairly contented. It is whether you would want to become the kind of self who is driven to find contentment on these terms. Choosing to become a self who is able to disregard the interests of other people means choosing to set yourself apart from the community and its judgments. However, many of your ideas of what it is to be fully human will come from developed traditions of your community. An uncritical rejection of those norms is likely to result in a self you have difficulty admiring.

To the extent that we are clear-headed about the choice of a self, we need to consider whether the unconstrained self is a self we can aspire to have. Does the thought of becoming a person who can feel no grief at causing others to suffer seem pleasing? Do we like the idea of being someone who lets down others when they are most dependent? Does the possibility of being a self able to take advantage of the weak and vulnerable seem attractive? Most of us find our identification with communal values to be strong enough to shape our sense of the kind of self we could aspire to become. If there are those who could be pleased with being antisocial selves, they are likely to strike most of us as suffering from some severe incapacity rather than as selves whose liberation from conventional living is worthy of emulation.

INTERNALIZED LIMITS

Being an honest person means not having to deliberate on each occasion about whether to behave honestly. In one sense eliminating options that another person might consider is a limit on the pursuit of self-interest. However, it is sometimes a profound relief to have your options limited by a firm sense of who you are and what you stand for. Having principles which are built into your identity and are not up for grabs every time a decision needs to be made can provide a stability and unity to one's life that is personally satisfying. The person without settled principles may struggle with issues that have been decided in advance for the person of principle.

Think, for example, of the married man who has a strong sense of himself as a faithful spouse. Given this self-image, there is no need to consider every desirable and available female as a possible sexual partner. The husband's sense of his own identity can take some decisions off the table, for he regards some issues as settled and nonnegotiable. Of course, the person who finds this particular image unappealing will find such a limitation constraining. But it need not be constraining for the person whose identity is formed in part by the ideal of a faithful spouse. The point is not that internalized principles render one invulnerable to possible temptation. Rather it is that having an identity which includes particular limits may provide considerable satisfaction for a person without seeming confining at all. Living out your own ideal can feel like genuine freedom which you would be reluctant to exchange.

One who has internalized particular moral principles has a strong incentive to live in accordance with those principles. To identify with a picture of yourself as, for example, a person of your word invests occasions when you give your word with high stakes. Failing to live out your image of yourself is failing to be true to your own conception of what you want to be, and to engage in such behavior can lead to severe disappointment with yourself, at least if you are able to own up to what you have done. For persons who have internalized particular moral limits, the question of whether others will find out is often less fundamental than the question of whether the action allows them to maintain their own self-image and self-respect.

COUNTING THE COSTS

Can you get away with murder? Or with dishonesty? Or with taking advantage of the vulnerable? Sometimes you can, if you are willing to accept the costs. In many cases those costs seem so intangible that they appear not to carry much weight compared to goods like a new car or a prestigious job or an honored reputation. We are drawn toward the obvious payoff and find it difficult to take seriously a loss like damage to our character.

Furthermore, in any particular case where we are tempted by an immediate payoff which is in tension with the identity we are trying to maintain, we are prone to tell ourselves that this one time won't change our fundamental nature. I am still basically an honest person despite my willingness to accept a questionable kickback, still a good scientist despite fudging the data on an important experiment. However, our choices form the self who will be making the next choice, and what seems like an isolated aberration often reveals one's developing character. How we respond to strong pressure to compromise our ideals shows how much these ideals are really a part of our identity.

The ancient philosopher, Plato, thought that the problem with treating other people unjustly was that it revealed a self that is out of control, one in which the desiring element dictated an individual's behavior, overruling the person's judgment. I argued in Chapter Three that the interpretation of "getting what you want" which makes the most sense involves tempering desires in accordance with one's reflectively chosen conception of a desirable life. So we might take Plato's claim to be that a repudiation of moral restraints is a matter of allowing unreflective impulses free rein instead of shaping those impulses by reflective judgment about the way you want to live.

We can dispute whether this is always the case or whether it might be reasonable for someone to choose a conception of a desirable life which excluded or minimized moral restraint. However, most of us are going to find that the kind of life we want requires an identity which is shaped by particular moral ideals that presuppose internalized restraints. Insofar as we seek to live a life with that sort of identity, it is in our interest to act in ways which are consistent with maintaining the identity we aspire to possess.

While choosing to build into yourself certain moral constraints can be entirely reasonable, it is not without risks. To become the kind of person who is motivated by principle means being willing to act on the basis of principle even when doing so means personal sacrifice. The person whose ideal image of herself includes the character trait of truthfulness will have occasions in which it would be much more convenient to shade the truth in self-serving ways. The person who thinks of himself as loyal will experience times when a disloyal act would bring numerous benefits. But becoming a self whose identity is formed by particular ideals means becoming the kind of person who cannot easily lay aside the ideals for the sake of immediate advantage. Choosing to become such a self means giving up some options which might be available to you if you were a different self.

Would it be possible to choose an identity in which moral ideals would usually govern behavior, but could be set aside when the demands became too great? Could one aspire to be honest, but not too honest, or to be a person of her word, as long as it does not become too difficult? Undoubtedly, this is the kind of compromise that many people try to make. However, it is at best a shaky compromise, for the ideal has very little to do with the identity it is supposed to shape. What one is asking for is an identity shaped by a fundamental concern with personal benefits plus the comfort that a self-image of a different kind might provide. But being willing to violate your commitments when it serves your purposes is a strong indication that you are not the kind of person for whom the keeping of commitments is all that important.

Former United Nations Secretary-General, Dag Hammarskjöld, may have had in mind the illusion that we can pay lip service to moral ideals without allowing them to penetrate deeply when he concluded in his personal journal, "You cannot play with the animal in you without becoming wholly animal, play with falsehood without forfeiting your right to truth, play with cruelty without losing your sensitivity of mind. He who wants to keep his garden tidy doesn't reserve a plot for weeds."[7]

The point is that governance by a reflectively chosen conception of a desirable life can be quite precarious. Unless our conception is given the authority to shape and direct conflicting impulses, we may end up with a kind of anarchy in which our real identity is something other than what we have reflectively chosen. Ultimately it is the choices we make that define who we are. Little choices and big ones form an identity that is often at variance with the self we think we are or hope to be. Becoming the self we have chosen, rather than some other self requires a kind of vigilance in which our vision of what we stand for guards against forces that would pull us in other directions.

Of course, we do not have to stand for anything. But it is risky to assume that just any self we happen to form will be one that we can respect or care about. Loving yourself may seem like something that happens automatically, but in fact our ability to love ourselves probably depends on maintaining the kind of self we can recognize as worth loving.[8] When we count the costs of behavior in tension with our ideals, the costs which seem intangible, perhaps hardly worth considering, may turn out to be the most important of all.

Chapter Seven

THE DEVELOPED SELF

Next to selfishness, the principal cause which makes life unsatisfactory is a want of mental cultivation. A cultivated mind...finds sources of inexhaustible interest in all that surrounds it...(John Stuart Mill[1])

It would be for most of us a highly disagreeable experience to meet, in the flesh, our future selves. Not just for the visual shock of seeing our own spirits animating bent limbs, watery eyes, and sagging jowls; but for the moral shock of meeting individuals whom we have daily and disgracefully wronged. (Robert Grudin[2])

One of the difficulties involved in choosing how to live is that we have only a partial understanding of the options available to us.[3] This limitation of understanding arises not merely because we have failed to work hard enough at acquiring information. It results from the fact that some ways of life would involve changing ourselves, and often we have only an obscure idea of what it would be like to experience things from the point of view of the changed self. I might aspire to be a musician, but I cannot really comprehend a musician's experiences if I do not have the kind of aesthetic sensibilities that musical training could develop in me. I might wonder what it would be like to become a philosopher, but unless I actually go through the process which will train me to think philosophically, I will have only vague intimations of what such a life would be like. Choosing to develop ourselves in a particular way is not exactly a shot in the dark, but neither is it typically a choice between fully understood options.

A dramatic illustration of this point can be found in Willy Russell's play, *Educating Rita*. At the beginning of the play Rita, an intelligent young woman from a working-class background, is seeking to break out of the confines of the kind of life she has been socialized to accept. She is twenty-six years old, but has resisted the typical pattern of having babies as expected by her husband and her family because she wants to "discover" herself. To achieve this aim, she enrolls in an Open University literature curriculum. Rita's assigned tutor is a cynical and drunken professor (Frank) who finds in her spontaneous and unaffected straightforwardness a breath of fresh air.

Rita recognizes that the world she hopes to enter is one which she neither fits into nor comprehends. The professor, who is at home in the world of liberally educated people, published a critically acclaimed book of poetry years ago, but has done nothing of consequence in his field since. He has given up on discovering much of value in life and lost whatever engagement he once had with his discipline, finding his primary solace in drink.

Rita wants to reach the level of performance of Frank's regular daytime students, but there is a vast cultural gap separating her from the kind of sophisticated reading and critical thinking that they are able to do. At one point she asks Frank to evaluate her essay on *Macbeth*. Frank is reluctant. He found in her essay a passionate description of her emotional reaction to the play. Taken in its own terms, it is a sincere, even moving, account of what she experienced when she saw the play performed. But in terms of the kind of critical thinking needed to pass exams, her essay is worthless. Rita presses Frank to tell her what to do to think and write like the other students:

> **Frank:** But if you're going to write this sort of stuff you're going to have to change.
> **Rita:** All right. Tell me how to do it.
> **Frank:** (*getting up*) But I don't know if I want to tell you Rita, I don't know that I want to teach you. (*He moves towards the desk)* What you already have is valuable.
> **Rita:** Valuable? What's valuable? The only thing I value is here, comin' here once a week.
> **Frank:** But, don't you see, if you're going to write this sort of thing—(*he indicates the pile of essays*)—to pass examinations, you're going to have to suppress, perhaps even aban-

> don your uniqueness. I'm going to have to change you.
> **Rita:** But don't you realize, I want to change.[4]

From Rita's perspective there is scarcely a choice to be made. Her dissatisfaction with her current life has made her willing to do whatever it takes to move toward what she is convinced will be a better kind of life. She has found a value in reading and discussing literary works which makes her other activities seem valueless by comparison. Even if she does not fully understand what kind of change this study will involve, she is convinced that it will be an improvement. As she thinks about what she has and what she wants, there is little question in her mind that she desires to become the new person these studies will make of her.

Ironically, it is the professor who is reluctant. Frank can easily do the kind of thinking and writing that Rita now aspires to do, but he wonders if the person she might become would have lost just those characteristics he finds most valuable in her. The world which she finds alien, but alluring, is one which he experiences as empty and unsatisfying, and he is unsure that the kind of mental discipline needed to discuss literature critically will improve her life. It is not a question of whether he can bring about the change in Rita; it is a question of whether he should.

RITA'S CHOICE

Rita's decision to develop her mind by pursuing a literary education is made against the backdrop of her dissatisfaction with the pattern of life she has been socialized to accept. On her account the values implicit in her life were formed under a kind of peer pressure not to take schooling or study seriously and to think of it as useless. The real concerns were "music an' clothes and lookin' for a feller ..." Rita's attempt to find satisfaction in the prescribed mode of life leads her to question it:

> Not that I went along with it so reluctantly. I mean, there was always somethin' in me head, tappin' away, tellin' me I might have got it all wrong. But I'd just play another record or buy another dress an' stop worryin'. There's always

> somethin to make you forget about it. So y' do, y' keep goin', tellin' yourself life's great. There's always another club to go to, a new feller to be chasin', a laugh an' a joke with the girls. Till, one day y' own up to yourself an' say, is this it? Is this the absolute maximum I can expect from this livin' lark? An' that's the big moment that one, that's the point when y' have to decide whether it's gonna be another change of dress or a change in yourself. An' it's really temptin' to go out an' get another dress y' know, it is. Cos it's easy, it doesn't cost anythin', it doesn't upset anyone around y'. Like cos they don't want y' to change.[5]

Later in describing "working-class culture" Rita doubts that anyone living this kind of life can really be content:

> Cos there's no meanin'. They tell y' stories about the past, y' know the war, or when they were fightin' for food an' clothin' an' houses. Their eyes light up as they tell y' because there was some meanin' to it. But the thing is now, I mean now that most of them have got some sort of house an' there's food an' money around, they know they're better off but, honest, they know they've got nothin' as well.[6]

Rita attempts to communicate her discontent to her husband, but he cannot understand what she is looking for beyond a house in a better neighborhood. What she is looking for is metaphorically summed up in an account of a scene in a pub where family and friends are singing a song they learned from the juke-box. Rita, having sensed how far she is from entering the world of the educated, has decided to give up the attempt. So she joins in the singing, but notices that her mother had stopped singing and begun to cry. At first she won't say why, but on the way home when Rita asks her, she replies, "... because we could sing better songs than those."[7]

Rita's dissatisfaction with the kind of life she is living leads her to look for a life with better songs. She comes to believe that the door to such a life is to be found in the education she is seeking. While there is unrealistic idealization in her grasp of an alternative type of life, she is attracted by what she can understand of its exemplars, and as she attempts to enter this alien culture, she finds something which engages her attention and excites her. There are enough intimations of the kind of satisfaction she seeks to draw her in. Her dissatisfaction with the kind of life she had been living, combined with this promising alternative of a better life, is enough to convince her that she needs to develop the capacities which will make this new life possible.

The kind of thinking that Rita's choice rests on could be described as a reflection on her life as a whole. She is not merely trying to satisfy her existing desires. Rather, she is assuming a perspective from which she can evaluate these desires. As she thinks about her life as a whole, Rita judges many of the things which occupied her attention and effort to be empty and superficial. While it was easy enough to get caught up in these pursuits, she finds that from a reflective distance she cannot endorse the kind of life they entail. In rejecting the values underlying her activities, Rita rejects the kind of self able to live such a life. Her reflective judgment leads her to seek for a different life and a different self.

The alternative type of life which appeals to Rita is one in which she develops her mind through an understanding of great literature. She has only the vaguest understanding of what educated people are like, yet she judges their interests and concerns to be superior to her own. She cannot fully imagine what it would be like to be one of these people, but the interests that her study arouses, and the satisfaction she begins to feel create a strong attraction to what seems like a better kind of life.

EDUCATION AND LIFE-TRANSFORMATION

Rita's attempt to improve her life through educational development may strike some people as odd. Often people think of education as a way to gain knowledge or skills (or credentials) that will enable them to achieve specific goals such as getting a better job or making more money. However, Rita's interest in studying literature has no immediate connection with any vocational plans. She thinks that the educational experience will enhance the quality of her life, regardless of what she does for a living. Studying and learning to discuss literary works are ways of developing her mind, and she sees this sort of intellectual development as an important element in the kind of life she aspires to have.

How might the type of intellectual development Rita seeks affect the quality of her life? One very significant result we might expect is an enlargement of her world. Rita is familiar with the beliefs and practices of the local community in which she grew up. She knows what that community expects of people, what role deviations are allowed, and what efforts will win social approval and encouragement. Her education will introduce her to ideas, practices, and values from other places and other times. The literary works she studies will make her aware of ways of thinking and living that will enlarge her imaginative capacities and enable her to consider her own beliefs and norms from a wider perspective. She will acquire new concepts and new frameworks as she thinks about and discusses literary works. These new ways of thinking will challenge her self-understanding, but they will also bring unexpected insights into the realities and possibilities of living.

Accompanying this kind of intellectual enlargement, Rita's studies are likely to sharpen her capacities for critical judgment. She will learn to judge some ideas and interpretations as half-baked or ill-considered, while recognizing others as worthy of more serious consideration. As she struggles to understand, lines of thought which seemed initially promising will be revealed as blind alleys. But there will also be discoveries, some she arrives at on her own and some with the aid of more experienced thinkers. As she exercises her critical faculties, Rita can be expected to increase her capacity to judge what to accept and what to reject in the enlarged world she has entered. Furthermore, the powers of critical thought acquired through her studies will become a part of her, shaping her judgment in all her activities.

Along with critical judgment, Rita's studies will train her aesthetic tastes. Before her venture into education, her reading diet consisted largely of popular pulp fiction. As she is exposed to works of literature, Rita begins to acquire a taste for literary works, eventually learning to distinguish between formula fiction and works of literary worth, and later between good works and great ones. Rita's awakened aesthetic sensitivities can be expected to penetrate her awareness of her everyday experiences, changing what she notices, and altering her judgments of worth as well as her choices.

Related to developing capacities for critical and aesthetic judgment is an enriched capacity for empathetic understanding. The kind of education Rita is pursuing should make her aware of how much she can learn from points of view which differ from her own. If her education is successful, she will learn that the impulse to reject strange-sounding ideas out of hand often results in superficial understanding and superficial criticisms. By contrast she should find that efforts to comprehend the full strength of positions that seem wrong, to feel the attractions of those positions, are necessary for giving telling critiques, and that often such deep understandings will reveal some things worth accepting. Rita's education should instill in her a habit of empathetic listening which can transform her relationships as well as deepening her awareness and understanding of her own convictions.

The educational experience Rita seeks will bring her into contact with a vast tradition which includes some of the most profound thinkers and most creative minds of our civilization. We might compare her exposure to this tradition to entering a conversation with people from a wide geographical and temporal span. If Rita retains an openness to learning from this enlarged conversational circle, she will not remain the same. Her beliefs will be altered as she takes account of ideas and perspectives she had not considered. Her values will change in the light of her awareness of attractive alternatives to her own ways of living. Even the nature of her experiences will be altered. As she encounters poetic portrayals of human living, she is likely to discover, not just new words for expressing what she is already experiencing, but paradigms and images which open the door to a fuller range and greater depth of experience.

DOES INTELLECTUAL DEVELOPMENT IMPROVE A PERSON'S LIFE?

It is tempting to say that the changes produced by Rita's education will improve her life, and that is clearly her expectation. But should we think of this sort of educational development as leading generally to a better sort of life? A classic discussion by John Stuart Mill bears on this question. Mill distinguishes between the kinds of bodily pleasures that human beings share with lower animals and those enjoyments that come from development of distinctively human capacities. He argues that a life in which a person's intellectual, aesthetic, and moral capacities are developed and exercised can be judged superior to a life which neglects these capacities. The basis for this claim is an imagined comparison by the only kind of individual who is competent to judge: someone who has an understanding of what both kinds of life would be like. The only person capable of such understanding, says Mill, will be someone who has developed the capacities in question and knows what it means to use them. When we turn to such an individual for a verdict, we will discover that "... those who are equally acquainted with and equally capable of appreciating and enjoying both do give a most marked preference to the manner of existence which employs their higher faculties."[8]

The conclusion that Mill attributes to his experienced judge is *not* that a life employing the "higher" faculties will be more pleasurable or contain more satisfaction than a life devoted to bodily pleasure. Mill acknowledges that the person who is occupied with sensual appetites might find such a life fully satisfying and that the cultivation of the capacities for intellectual and aesthetic satisfactions might actually increase the total amount of dissatisfaction. Nevertheless, he thinks, the superiority of the more developed life may be seen from the following thought experiment:

> Few human creatures would consent to be changed into any of the lower animals for a promise of the fullest allowance of the beast's pleasures; no intelligent human being would consent to be a fool, no instructed person would be an ignoramus, no person of feeling and conscience would

> be selfish and base, even though they should be persuaded that the fool, the dunce, or the rascal is better satisfied with his lot than they are with theirs. They would not resign what they possess more than he for the complete satisfaction of all the desires they have in common with him.[9]

If we take Mill to be appealing merely to the unwillingness to give something up, it is not clear how this unwillingness could show one mode of life superior to another. Suppose someone tells me that if I undertake a particular program of meditation, I will become unconcerned with worldly values and develop a strong desire for a simple and ascetic lifestyle. Suppose I become convinced on the basis of observing others who have undertaken the same program that this claim is very likely true and, furthermore, that if I complete this program, I would not trade the kind of life I have achieved for any combination of the worldly pleasures I now pursue. The testimony of my possible future self may still not be enough to convince me that this program is the path to a better life.

However, my reluctance to grant authority to the judgments of a possible future self probably results from a skepticism about whether this self fully appreciates the kind of life I now have. I might wonder whether the point of view produced by this process would undermine this person's capacity for giving the prior life its due. In Mill's argument this problem is circumvented by a stipulation that the person who has developed intellectual, aesthetic, and moral capacities has a complete understanding of what human satisfactions are available without these capacities. Hence, if we accept the stipulation, there is reason to regard the judgments of the fully informed evaluator as carrying significant authority.

On what grounds, however, are these judgments made? Mill makes it clear that the basis for judging one mode of life inferior to another is that it does not measure up to a conception of happiness that anyone acquainted with both modes would have to accept. He claims,

> ... a beast's pleasures do not satisfy a human being's con-

> ception of happiness. Human beings have faculties more elevated than the animal appetites and, when once made conscious of them, do not regard anything as happiness which does not include their gratification.[10]

So the unwillingness to sacrifice a particular type of development is an unwillingness to give up something which is regarded as essential to happiness. Mill is saying that a conception of happiness or fulfillment for a human being will include an implicit standard of human development which can be used to evaluate the place of various satisfactions within an individual life. When we assume this evaluative perspective, we will judge some ways of living as more fully developed, and others will be so undeveloped as to be found unworthy of us as human beings.

What Mill calls a conception of happiness might be equated to what I called in Chapter Three a conception of a desirable life. There I claimed that when we develop such conceptions, we have a basis for judging particular desires and goals in terms of how well they fit into the overall conception. This sort of evaluation allows us to arrange our various wants in hierarchical fashion, recognizing some of them as more fundamental to the kind of life we are trying to achieve. Some elements in the hierarchy will function as bottom-line conditions for any life we could regard as worthy or fulfilling.

Notice, however, that the judgments of value which Mill finds inevitable for the fully informed individual are quite general. A happy life includes some mental development, but this is not to say that the life of the scholar is preferable to the life of a business executive. As long as we stick to contrasts between the life of a beast or a fool and the life of Socrates, we have little difficulty judging that one has and the other lacks something essential to the human good. But considering the varieties of possible human development, we could not use this kind of argument to be very precise about what type of development would be best for a particular individual. There may be limits on the kinds of life which we could recognize as fulfilling for human beings, but there is room for significant variety within those limits.

DEVELOPMENT AND IDENTITY

When a particular individual, such as Rita, attempts to think about what is needed for a desirable life, she should consider, not just general facts about human nature, but what will be fulfilling for someone with her particular talents, inclinations and social opportunities. In the context of Russell's play, her educational pursuits are a means to her general goal of "discovering" herself. Presumably this means that she wants to follow her own reflectively chosen aspirations rather than living a life dictated by social expectations. Education is the path that will allow her to become aware of who she wants to be.

In the play we are given a series of snapshots of Rita before and after the transformation her education produces. She gradually acquires greater self-confidence, becoming pleased with herself as she enters the world that had initially been so alien. The contrast between Rita in the first act and in the last is so remarkable that Rita appears to be an altogether different person. Yet the lingering question is whether these changes amount to an improvement

Frank had hesitated about whether to produce the change that Rita asked for, and once the change has occurred, he has reason to question whether he did the right thing. As Rita learns to fit in, she adopts for a time an affected manner of speech which she takes to be the way educated people talk. She falls under the influence of some trendy ways of thinking adopted from influential friends. When Frank contemplates the results of his creation, he compares himself to Frankenstein. Rita takes his concerns to be misguided. She says,

> ... what you can't bear is that I am educated now...I've got what you have an' y' don't like it because you'd rather see me as the peasant I once was...I've got a room full of books. I know what clothes to wear, what wine to buy, what plays to see, what papers and books to read. I can do without you.[11]

Frank replies,

> Is that all you wanted? Have you come all this way for so very, very little?...Found a culture have you, Rita? Found a better song to sing have you? No—you've found a different song, that's all...[12]

One version of Frank's criticism is that Rita's initial goal to discover herself has not been achieved. She has merely substituted the values absorbed from a new crowd for the values she had received from an earlier one. She fits in with the new group, but the superficial marks of fitting in are remarkably similar to those which enabled her to fit with her previous friends. There is little sign that her new way of life has brought the fulfillment she had hoped for. She has still not come to terms with the question of who she is.

Earlier I described the kind of thinking Rita does when she chooses to develop her mind as a reflection on her life as a whole. Her reflection focuses on what she finds unsatisfactory about her life, and in the rush to repudiate her past life and start a new one, she does not stop to consider what she wants to retain and what values she will regard as nonnegotiable aspects of her identity. Hence, she becomes susceptible to an unreflective imitation of her new friends.

The educational process gives Rita an enhanced ability to think about and evaluate her life. But Rita must make use of these powers, if she is to achieve her initial goal. The reflection she needs will inevitably be a process. She cannot expect to form her identity in a single afternoon. She will need to adjust her thinking as new possibilities become clearer. But she needs to come to some realization of what she regards as important and what pattern of life will fit with her unique talents and opportunities. Only then will she fulfill her original aim of self-discovery.

POSSIBLE SELVES

There are many possible selves that each of us might become. No one can develop every capacity. In building a conception of a desirable life we have to choose what specific kinds of development to make a part of our core identity. Some choices are revocable, and we learn as we go, attempting to adjust the self we have produced into a coherent whole. However, earlier choices establish limits. Though I might have developed my musical aptitudes in my twenties, becoming a world-class violinist, a failure to do so can remove this option as a realistic possibility in later life.

We do not choose from the position of the fully knowledgeable evaluator in Mill's thought experiment. Instead we rely on the bits of knowledge available to us. Often examples of a particular type of development are crucial to the formation of our aspirations. Learning of the professor who dazzled the mathematical world with a solution of Fermat's last theorem may resonate deeply in someone's unformed desires. Observing a mother who left an indelible impression on her highly successful children may evoke an admiration which is put to work in imitation. The examples we encounter give us a concrete understanding of possibilities we might develop in ourselves.

Recently I attended a memorial service for a friend who had died. Liz Ann was in her seventies, and we knew that she had been diagnosed with leukemia, but it was supposed to be the kind that would leave her years of life. However, she caught pneumonia, and what we expected to be a short stay in the hospital turned into an ordeal in the intensive care unit. It was heartbreaking to see a woman so full of life, rendered unconscious and sustained by medical technology until the efforts were clearly futile.

The church holding the memorial service was packed with friends and relatives who had been touched by Liz Ann's influence. Several spoke publicly about various aspects of her life, and their words described characteristics that were easily recognizable to those who had known her. One person spoke of her artistic sensitivities. She had been a skilled artist whose work was widely appreciated. She had also been instrumental in encouraging and creating opportunities for younger artists through leadership roles in the local art association.

Another person spoke of her dedication to her church. She was a key member in a regular prayer group, and for over twenty-five years she had taught a large adult Bible class composed of a diverse group of people who differed greatly in their theological ideas. She managed to create a congenial atmosphere among this group, welcoming open expression of divergent opinions, while still making clear her own firm convictions.

Another speaker emphasized Liz Ann's remarkable interpersonal skills. She had a striking ability to notice and affirm value in people she met. Many of us could echo the speaker's claim that when you talked to her, you felt as if you were the most valuable person in the world. Her interest was spontaneous and sincere, built on an unusual ability to empathize with others and perceive their strengths.

There were also stories of eccentricities, laughable incidents that brought out her uniqueness. But all in all, the service was a celebration of a life well lived. More than one person I talked to later said that the experience was a cause of personal reflection. Some of us wondered what people would say about us at our funeral, and several were inspired to work at developing their own skills in areas where Liz Ann's example made them feel deficient.

The point of this example is not just that some people do noteworthy things. It is that many of the things we admire in others are a reflection of how they have developed particular talents and skills that could have been neglected. Becoming someone with the ability to touch others in the way Liz Ann did is not an achievement that one should expect to perfect on the first try. It is the result of disciplined exercise of aptitude and attention. Some of us have more raw ability in certain areas than others, but in the end there is more than raw ability needed to develop the skills we admire most.

Robert Grudin notes how easy it is to forget about how our present action or inaction is producing a future self. He writes,

> If we did simple exercises for thirty minutes a day, we would greatly improve our strength, health, beauty and life expectancy. If we studied for one hour a day, we could relatively soon learn languages, master wide knowledge and develop new professions. If we sensibly invested $1 a day, we would in thirty years control substantial wealth. If we did ourselves the almost absurdly simple honor of planning

> our free time, we would enlarge ourselves into a whole new dimension of freedom.[13]

Recognizing the importance of ordering our daily activities is unlikely unless we form the habit of reflecting on our lives and becoming aware of the possible selves we are developing or failing to develop. Only then can we gain clarity about the significance of apparently trivial moments. Those moments can add up to a self that is grossly unformed in ways our considered judgment would deplore.

Grudin suggests that we think about what we are doing each moment in terms of the wrongs we may do to a future self. Our future self is at our mercy. We have the power to improve or to weaken this self by our present action or inaction. Grudin warns,

> It would be for most of us a highly disagreeable experience to meet, in the flesh, our future selves. Not just for the visual shock of seeing our own spirits animating bent limbs, watery eyes, and sagging jowls; but for the moral shock of meeting individuals whom we have daily and disgracefully wronged.[14]

If we think of our possible future selves in terms of self-interest, it is abundantly clear that in choosing particular forms of development, we are altering our interests. The person who has cultivated her capacity for enjoying scientific research now has an interest in doing research that her earlier self lacked. The individual who has nurtured a talent for entertaining others has an interest in exercising this skill that did not exist before it was developed. We can attempt to assess the interests of a self that has developed in a particular way, but self-interested thinking will not be sufficient to tell us which self to develop.

For that we need to reflect on what we admire, what we regard as important, and how this can be connected with our own unique possibilities. Once we have articulated the aspirations that specify what improvements we will seek, we can say that it is in our interest to do what it takes to produce that improved self. But unless we have reflectively chosen from among the many possibilities what capacities we will strive to develop in our future self, our self-interested thinking will lack the direction it needs in guiding our choices.

The kind of mindset which focuses our attention on obtaining particular benefits is different from the mindset in which we attend to what we are becoming and whether the capacities we are forming will produce the kind of life we want. When we evaluate the pursuit of benefits in the light of our more fundamental aims, it sometimes becomes clear that pursuing the benefits we are attracted to, either in the short-term or in the long-term, will undermine our efforts at self-transformation. Though it might seem we are pursuing our self-interest, we can wind up pursuing the interests of the wrong self. To put the pursuit of self-interest on track, we must discover how to claim as our own the manner of living that will create the self we have chosen to become.

Chapter Eight

THE ENGAGED SELF

When people say they need to find themselves, often what they really mean is that they want a meaningful life. (Roy Baumeister[1])

The pursuit of self-interest, as standardly conceived, is a life without any meaning beyond our own pleasure and satisfaction. (Peter Singer[2])

It is by being fully involved with every detail of our lives, whether good or bad, that we find happiness... (Mihaly Csikszentmihalyi[3])

Life is not a spectator sport. To achieve the life we want, we need to be fully engaged participants, caring deeply, sometimes even passionately, about the goals we pursue. We need to discover activities that capture our interest and ignite our imagination. We need to find projects and commitments that we can wholeheartedly embrace. In short, we need something to live for.

However, we are also reflective beings. Sometimes we need to stand back and consider our activities, examining the concerns that engage us and the goals that energize us. We need to be able to judge that the things occupying our attention and animating our imagination are worthwhile. In other words, we need to assure ourselves that what we are living for is something that matters.

While the dual stances of engagement and reflection are both important, they exist in some tension with each other. We cannot be moved to action by our concerns and commitments at the same time that we are pulling back to reflect on them. Effective engagement often requires us to put our reflective urges on hold lest they disrupt the active pursuit of our goals and interests. Imagine, for example, a gymnast who is preoccupied during competition with thoughts about whether all the hard work and sacrifice are worth it. Or worse, imagine someone who tries to occupy an evaluative stance regarding his technique while making love. Our moments of reflection produce a kind of disengagement which is incompatible with being fully involved in many of life's activities.

However, the tension between engagement and reflection arises, not merely because the activity of reflection interferes with engagement. Sometimes the results of reflection deflate the impulses that motivate certain pursuits. A person who once found great amusement in telling or listening to racist jokes, on encountering strong reasons for questioning the practice, may discover that this questioning has robbed the activity of much of its attraction. An aspiring novelist who takes to heart strong criticism from an editor might find that her zest for writing has withered away. In general, being able to evaluate our activities reflectively and to alter our behavior in the light of our reflective judgment is a good thing. But what if our reflection leads us to a negative judgment about virtually everything we do?

REFLECTIVE DISENGAGEMENT

Such was the experience of the great Russian novelist Leo Tolstoy at one point in his life. In an autobiographical account entitled, *A Confession*, Tolstoy describes how at the height of his powers, despite great fame and wealth, he was plunged into deep despair. He had been educated into the Christian faith as a child, but by the age of eighteen, he had discarded any religious belief. He had been fairly content with his life until his late forties when he began to reflect on the question of whether life has any meaning. His reflections led him to the conclusion that life was meaningless, and all his activities and pursuits were meaningless as well. He writes,

> My life came to a standstill. I could breathe, eat, drink and sleep and I could not help breathing, eating, drinking and sleeping; but there was no life in me because I had no desires whose gratification I would have deemed it reasonable to fulfill. If I wanted something I knew in advance that whether or not I satisfied my desire nothing would come of it.[4]

What Tolstoy describes is a kind of disengagement from his own life that undermined his ability to desire anything. It is as if he is going through the motions of living while his reflective self casts a critical eye on all his activities, rejecting his former assumptions about value and importance. Tolstoy says,

> If a magician had come and offered to grant my wishes I would not have known what to say. If in my intoxicated moments I still had the habit of desire, in my sober moments I knew that it was a delusion and that I wanted nothing. I did not even wish to know the truth because I had guessed what it was. The truth was that life was meaningless.[5]

Tolstoy's state of mind is an extreme one, but the line of thought he pursues bears some resemblance to the kind of thinking many people have experienced at times in their lives. Sometimes people develop a sense of futility about their activities because of repetitive aspects of life: "I get up, eat, go to work, come home, watch television, go to bed, and get up again. Is there any point to it all, or is life just a meaningless cycle of activities?" Accomplishments may produce a similar mode of thought. Suppose an individual achieves some goal in life that had seemed important. He worked long and hard to graduate with honors or become a vice president of the company, but when the goal is finally achieved, he finds that its value has disappeared. Or such reflection might come about when a person loses something which had been central to her life. A concert pianist develops crippling arthritis, and when her playing is taken away, she doubts whether anything worthwhile is left. In these and other kinds of situations, people stand back and reflect on their own activities, questioning their value, perhaps even questioning whether life is worth living.

Tolstoy's questioning was apparently instigated when he began to reflect on the fact of death. He came to a vivid awareness of what he had known intellectually, that death would come one day. When it did, Tolstoy reasoned,

> ...nothing will remain other than stench and worms. Sooner or later my deeds, whatever they have been, will be forgot-

> ten and will no longer exist. What is all the fuss about them? How can a person carry on living and fail to perceive this?[6]

What is it about the prospect of death that troubles Tolstoy so much? It is the incongruity between the passionate concerns which allowed him to be seriously engaged with life and the picture of what reality will be like after his death.[7] Viewing his life from a perspective that includes his death, Tolstoy finds that the things which had mattered so much to him in life lose their importance. Whatever he accomplished would eventually be destroyed. If he wrote great novels, they would in time be forgotten. If he cared for his family, they would some day be dead and gone. No matter what he did, he could not accomplish anything of lasting value. Once Tolstoy enters into this mode of thought, he finds it impossible to see the things which had engaged him as worth the effort.

The dreary conclusion he draws is not merely about his own life. Tolstoy thinks that what he has discovered about his life is true of everyone's life. The human plight, he says, is like that of a traveller who, trying to escape from a wild animal, jumps into a waterless well. Any thought of safety is short-lived, for he sees at the bottom of the well a dragon ready to swallow him. Since he does not dare to climb out, all he can do is grab hold of a piece of bush growing on the side of the well. Soon, however, his hands are growing weary, and when he looks around, he finds that two mice are nibbling away at the bush. There is no escape. At any moment the bush will give way: "The traveller sees this and knows he will inevitably perish. But while he is hanging there he sees some drops of honey on the leaves of the bush, stretches out his tongue and licks them."[8] For Tolstoy the two drops of honey were his family and his writing. For a while these interests had the power to divert his attention from his plight. But when he faces death directly, he can no longer find any sweetness in them. Instead he is driven to despair.

Why is the relative impermanence of his accomplishments so troubling for Tolstoy? We might compare his thinking to that of a man who gets up every day and builds a sand castle on the beach. Imagine that he builds elaborate sand castles with moats and towers and all sorts of interesting details. Each day when the tide comes in that day's castle is destroyed, and each day the man goes back to build a new one. We would not be too surprised if one day the man did not go to the beach and build a sand castle. He might reason that it would be pointless to go, since the castle will be destroyed before the day is over anyway.

While there are obviously things in life with greater permanence than sand castles, nothing seems to be absolutely permanent. Tolstoy's writings may last for thousands of years, but if one takes a long enough view, it is possible to see in them the same lack of any enduring value. Whether they last for a hundred years or a million years, they too are destined for destruction.

Clearly Tolstoy has set very high standards for the possibility of doing something worthwhile. Ordinarily we do recognize the endurance of achievements as having something to do with their value. Since we have only a limited amount of time to invest, we sometimes choose to direct our energies toward matters which hold some prospect for lasting achievements that will not soon disappear. Nevertheless, we usually recognize value in a great many things that are not absolutely permanent.

The difference between our ordinary judgments and those that Tolstoy is making appears to be a difference in perspective. Imagine comparing the accomplishments of a sand-castle builder whose works last less than a day to the accomplishments of a cathedral builder whose work may last thousands of years. From the ordinary human perspective we might encourage the sand-castle builder to devote his talents to something of more lasting value, such as cathedral building. Tolstoy takes a perspective from which all human activities, including cathedral building, amount to very little. He looks at human activities from what we might call a God's-eye viewpoint. From this perspective the achievements of the cathedral builder or the writer seem as transient as those of the sand-castle builder look from the ordinary human point of view. From Tolstoy's viewpoint the only satisfactory achievement would be something of eternal value.

FINDING MEANING

Tolstoy's worries about the meaninglessness of life are connected with his judgment that all activities are pointless. Consider an example of a pointless activity. A teacher assigns her class to make a list of every last name in the phone book with a third letter of m. The activity seems pointless because there is nothing of consequence to achieve by it. It is the kind of activity that is appropriately called busywork. To call it a pointless activity need not imply that the teacher had no reason for making the assignment. Perhaps she wanted to keep her students occupied. But such a purpose would not make the work meaningful for them. For class members to find the activity meaningful, they must become aware of some purpose of the activity that they can from their own perspective endorse as worthwhile.[9]

Similarly, to find meaning in our lives, we must be engaged in activities that we can connect with our judgments of what is valuable or important. Tolstoy's thought experiment shows us that it is possible to assume a point of view from which the significance of any of our accomplishments appears as microscopically small. What is unclear, however, is why that point of view should have the authority to cancel the recognition of value from every other viewpoint. Even if caring for the needs of my children seems like an insignificant accomplishment in the cosmic scheme of things, it could still be something that I judge to have real worth from a point of view that reflects my most considered judgments of what is valuable for a human being.

From the viewpoint of a member of the human species there are many potentially valuable pursuits. Enjoying a sunset, tending a garden, or memorizing a poem may be worthwhile experiences whether or not they contribute to any far-reaching ends. Developing a friendship or becoming a skilled counselor or composing a play may be projects that an individual can regard as worth a great deal of time and effort. Such activities need not be identified with the pointless busywork of the imagined teacher. They can be recognized as contributing to the kind of life a person might be pleased with from her own point of view.

Of course, putting together the sort of life we can judge

meaningful involves more than arranging some haphazard collection of worthwhile activities. When we reflect on our lives, we typically try to fit our various activities together as elements of a story. We habitually present ourselves to others by telling them parts of our story and listening to parts of their stories. The narrative form gives us a kind of interpretive framework which can be used to fit various elements together into some kind of coherent order.[10]

Some people's stories exhibit a thematic unity: a struggle to overcome a deplorable childhood, an early encounter with a dream that becomes a lifelong quest. Even when one's story is lacking in a central plot line, it may be given a unity through the characteristic style or concerns of the central character. A person with an attractive personality might make the focus of her life a series of nurturing personal relationships with individuals who are drawn to her. In one sense, developing a meaningful life is being able to organize the various elements together into a story that does justice to their reality and produces a satisfying unity.

However, what we find satisfying depends in part on whether we can judge the activities of the story's central character to be expressions of concerns for things that are genuinely important. It is possible to look at the story I have developed and find that I have devoted my life to matters which seem trivial from my own viewpoint about what is worth doing. While I need not conclude that my life has been worthless, I might very well think that it has been lacking in meaning. To have made it more meaningful, I needed to be moved to a much greater extent by concerns which differed from those which did move me. But since altering my concerns would alter my self, this amounts to saying that I needed to become a different self in order to live a more meaningful life.

MEANINGFUL ENGAGEMENT

Living a meaningful life calls for cultivating a self who cares enough about matters you can reflectively judge as important to allow those concerns to play a dominant role in shaping your actions. Typically there is some divergence between the values an individual claims to be hers and what we might infer to be valuable to her from observing her behavior. A person may say that family life is of great importance, yet allow a focus on career advancement to squeeze out significant attention to the family. One might claim to have a concern for contributing to the advancement of scientific truth, yet attempt to get by with carelessly designed experiments or fudged data. What a person really values is usually revealed more reliably in action than in high-sounding profession.

Since we are often unaware of the divergence between our professed values and those that are revealed in our patterns of conduct, we can unwittingly devote inordinate amounts of time to activities we judge to be lacking in significance. Most people seriously underestimate how much time they spend in activities such as watching television and how little time they spend in actions they would rate as higher priorities, such as conversation with family members. Essentially escapist activities can have a hypnotic effect, lulling us into a kind of passivity that effectively abdicates the control we might exercise over our own lives. When we allow our behavior to be molded by immediate inclinations that are at odds with our reflective values, we can easily find ourselves filling up the available hours with pursuits that fail to contribute to a life story we can regard as meaningful or significant.

People who do live meaningful lives are somehow able to be engaged by concerns that reflect their best judgments about what is worthwhile. Consider Suzie Valdez, for example.[11] Ms. Valdez has organized much of her life around efforts to provide food, clothing, and other basic needs of the poor children of Ciudad Juarez, a Mexican city across the border from El Paso. Known in the region as "Queen of the Dumps," she typically spends fourteen-hour days occupied with relief efforts conducted out of an old van. Single-handedly, she developed and organized a group of volunteers and solicited the aid of local businesses to deal with the most desperate poverty of Juarez.

Remarkably, Valdez began this effort as a single mother of four, without monetary resources and with only a slight knowledge of Spanish and a tenth grade education. Working at part-time jobs to provide her own family's basic necessities, she nevertheless threw herself into an exhausting and endless task that has consumed her energy for over thirty years. In the early years she struggled against a series of obstacles such as how to take medications past the border authorities and how to bury the children who died despite her efforts. For the latter problem she built homemade coffins from cardboard and thin plywood, transporting them in a borrowed van.

Suzie Valdez undertook her work with a religious sense of calling. She came to believe that God had given her a task which had to be done. In response to each obstacle she maintained a conviction that God would provide the means. Her efforts could not have been sustained, however, without deep personal concerns for those she helped. In response to questions from social scientists who attempted to understand her motivations, she said, "These are precious people.... The Lord has given me a love for these people that I myself don't understand."[12] Researchers were struck not only by her diligence and ingenuity in the face of numerous discouraging problems, but by what they called her "unmitigated joy." In her life they found

> a fundamental identification of the self with the values and beliefs that are at the heart of the work. She has become consumed by her work, fully and completely engaged. For Suzie, her work is her life. It makes her more fully alive ... As she sees it, the work with the poor of Juarez is what she is here for, and what she most wants to do.[13]

According to the researchers it is this unity between the self Valdez has developed and her basic values that accounts for her wholehearted desire to do what she is doing. In this unity they find "the key to her stamina, her certainty, and her joy."[14]

Suzie Valdez is a striking example of someone whose expressed values are in harmony with her actions. She has made those values so much a part of who she is that living a life other than one of service to God through aiding the poor has become unthinkable to her. She has built her fundamental concerns into her sense of her identity in a way that colors her perception of the world and its possibilities. The result is a self who can be fully engaged in the kinds of things she judges most important. She says, "The ministry is in my heart and I'll never leave it. I'll never want to leave it just because it keeps me humble. It keeps my perspective of life in the right order, and it keeps my priorities in line."[15]

SELF-INTEREST AND MEANING

It would be stretching language to call the conduct of Suzie Valdez self-interested. Her devotion to the poor has demanded considerable personal sacrifice, both for herself and for her children. If we try to conceive her calculating the potential costs and benefits to herself, it is difficult to imagine that she could have concluded that a life devoted to meeting the needs of the poor would provide her with greater benefit than alternative ways of living.

Nevertheless, the life she is living is one in which she finds great satisfaction. In fact, she cannot seriously consider any other way of living. The reason she gives is instructive: Her way of life coincides with her priorities. She is living in harmony with her judgments of what things are worth doing and of what kind of person she aspires to be. Given the kind of self she seeks to be, her judgments about her interest are inextricably combined with concerns about how best to meet the needs of the poor children she is dedicated to helping.

The self-interested point of view involves thinking about possible actions in terms of potential benefits to the self. However, when we start to think about living a meaningful life, it becomes apparent that a self focused on its own benefits is unlikely to achieve much meaning. This is because meaningful engagement hinges on doing things we can regard as significant or important, and our judgments of what is significant push us toward a context wider than the self. When I think that it is important for my need for health care to be met, I have little basis for refusing to admit that it is important for others to have their health care needs met too. If I think that some athletic goal would be a worthwhile accomplishment for me, I will be hard-pressed to deny the value of a similar accomplishment for someone else.

There is a kind of objectivity to judgments of importance that moves one's awareness beyond personal needs or concerns to a larger interpersonal context.

One consequence is that personal goals which do not transcend the self can seem insignificant in relation to the larger context. When my goals are exhausted by concerns for *my* success or *my* enjoyment, I may find that achieving them fails to satisfy my urge to do something worthwhile, for my thinking about what is worthwhile places me in a realm where something other than my own satisfaction matters. Only by developing a self whose concerns are linked to what I recognize as mattering can I live the kind of life I regard as meaningful.

If I do develop a self concerned about things beyond myself, I may find it necessary to give up some personal benefits I might otherwise have had. My service as a Big Brother may mean I have significantly less time available for leisure activities. My unpaid appointment to the governing board of my state's college system might mean the loss of substantial income I could have expected had I given the same time to my own business. In general, if I build into myself concerns that will lead to a more meaningful life, I will be acknowledging considerations in my decision-making that can compete with more purely personal concerns.

Such considerations emerge in extreme form in the life of Suzie Valdez where a dominant passion for her ministry has squeezed out concerns for her own comfort and security. Not every meaningful life involves such a high level of personal sacrifice. Some meaningful ways of life can allow more room for self-gratification. Even when personal sacrifice seems major to others, however, it may not appear that way to the person who is fully engaged by something transcending the self. For when the engagement expresses fundamental concerns of the self, it often means doing exactly what the person wholeheartedly wants to do.

Jeremy Bernstein describes in an autobiographical book about his early life how, despite unlikely beginnings, he went on to become a world-class physicist. In high school he took only one course in science and did only mediocre work in it. In his freshman year of college he attempted to complete the science requirement by taking the lowest-level science course, the one reserved for "basket cases in science." During this course Bernstein's curiosity was aroused, and eventually he majored in physics, going on to complete a doctorate and do distinguished research in the field. He sums up his engagement with the discipline as follows:

> Once I was pointed in the direction of physics, I became obsessed by the subject—drunk on it. That feeling is very hard to convey... The experiences I have been describing occurred in and around the interstices of my obsession with physics.[16]

For a person who has become obsessed or fully engaged in an enterprise that transcends the self, the time and effort devoted to that enterprise is unlikely to seem like a sacrifice. Bernstein devoted countless hours to research in physics because he had come to care about the discipline. Its problems energized his intellectual life and challenged him to put forth the kind of effort and creative thinking needed to solve them. His work on physics was an expression of concerns that had become part of him. A different self might look at the incredibly difficult demands of such devotion and think about all it means giving up. But someone who is pursuing projects that fully engage the self will be doing what he loves.

THE SELF AND REFLECTIVE VALUATION

Can our self-interested thinking tell us what kind of self to be? To think so is to fall into a confusion that I have been trying to combat in this book. Until I have formulated my aspirations, there is no such thing as the self it is most in my interest to be, though there may be plenty of selves it is not in my interest to be. Some selves may be incapable of fulfilling even the vaguely defined aspirations I will have without much reflection. But choosing a specific self is a matter of giving my aspirations a precise specification.

The choice of a self is not a matter of weighing and comparing predetermined benefits, since in choosing a self we are, in part, deciding what will count as benefits for us. We do this by judging what sort of life we are willing to identify with. One who reflects on this question will undoubtedly want to consider whether some imagined way of life would satisfy her. But asking what life would be satisfactory is very different from asking how to effectively satisfy existing desires, for when we think about possible selves, we are attempting to evaluate desires to determine whether they can be reflectively endorsed.

For example, suppose a person has built a life around the goal of achieving financial success. His dominant desire has been to make as much money as possible. Each achievement has been gratifying, but after each success there is a powerful urge to get more. While we can easily imagine such an individual as being too unreflective to devote a second thought to his way of life, we can also imagine a person who, standing back from his own life, finds his activities and the pattern of concerns they display to be empty and unfulfilling. Such an individual would be assessing his actual self from the point of view of a reflective self that feels the pull of evaluative categories that call his desires into question.

Asking such questions as, "What ways of living can I admire?" or "What kinds of pursuits accomplish something worthwhile?" potentially opens the door to answers which are inconvenient from the point of view of satisfying our existing desires. Our reflective capacities push us toward a perspective in which we see our current motivational pattern as one among many possibilities. Suppose that self-examination reveals that I am motivated by a strong desire for promiscuous sexual experience. My reflective capacities allow me to stand back and consider that desire to see whether I want to serve it or try to alter it. When I critically distance myself from my desires, thinking of whether the way of life they lead to is compatible with my most considered judgments of value, I am attempting to become clear about what motivations I am willing to make my own.

Our judgments of value are likely to reflect a perspective that transcends the self. David Hume claims that the character qualities we esteem are those which promote the happiness of the group rather than individual interests.[17] We admire benevolent or generous behavior, even though engaging in it may be personally inconvenient or even self-sacrificial. Hume thinks that these kinds of judgments are grounded in a common human nature which has social as well as self-interested sentiments. Whether he is right about that or not, it should be clear that when we try to think about what is valuable or worthy, we have to start with a vocabulary that is socially shaped. Our value terms are permeated with a social perspective, and when we try to formulate aspirations for the self, they will be very likely to incorporate concerns which are more impartial than a concern with self-interest alone could produce.

Choosing a self means taking seriously the human capacity to formulate values and to apply those values to our life. When we think about what way of living would be meaningful or noble or humane, we are engaging in a kind of disinterested reflection that allows us to form a conception of an ideal self that we will seek to become. Of course, this kind of thinking could result in an ideal self which is in significant conflict with the priorities apparent in one's actual way of life. While we can to some extent modify our ideals to bring them closer to the current behavioral realities, we cannot simply erase the values underlying them without suppressing something fundamental to our nature. The self whose interests we pursue needs to be brought into some harmony with the self of our reflective aspirations.

ATTRACTIVE POSSIBILITIES AND SELF-FORMATION

Although we may not be able to establish the superiority of one way of life to another by objectively weighing and comparing the benefits of each, we can sometimes be attracted by intimations of what a different way of life might have to offer. I may not know what it would be like to be obsessed with physics in the way Bernstein describes, but I have probably had experiences of something which captured my attention, at least temporarily. In fact, when I think about the kinds of experiences that I have found most enjoyable, they are likely to include instances in which I became so absorbed in doing something that I forgot myself.

Psychologist Mihaly Csikszentmihalyi calls experiences of this sort flow experiences. Flow is "the state in which people are so involved in an activity that nothing else seems to matter; the experience itself is so enjoyable that people will do it even at great cost, for the sheer sake of doing it."[18] From studying this kind of experience in artists, athletes, musicians, chess masters, and surgeons, Csikszentmihalyi found a remarkable similarity in the way they described their flow experiences. Experiences as diverse as rock climbing and heart surgery were characterized in terms of an intense concentration on the activity at hand that shut everything else out. This concentration was made possible by a clearly defined task demanding the exercise of skillful action. When the match between skill level and the task at hand was optimal, individuals described a sense of effortless involvement in which they lost awareness of time and the self, but felt a satisfying sense of control. These experiences involved an intense focus of psychic energy that people found immensely enjoyable and rewarding.

The flow experience is a special kind of engagement. One can be completely engaged in activity that expresses fundamental concerns and commitments while only occasionally experiencing flow. For instance, a writer who has a compelling interest in telling a story may find aspects of the work tedious. A teacher who is fully committed to the classroom may experience times of immense frustration and discouragement. Flow represents those moments when an individual's engagement slips into high gear, bringing into sharp focus a harmony between actor and activity.

Having experienced flow in games or athletic contests, a person might be able to form some idea of what it would be like to be fully engaged in a less familiar activity. For an outsider the passionate interest of an archeologist whose attention is focused on a delicate excavation of an ancient mound may seem a bit opaque. One who lacks a fascination with the details of ancient history that the archeological dig may reveal cannot fully enter into the frame of mind of the archeologist. But even the outsider can vaguely apprehend how someone who has internalized the relevant interests and concerns might be caught up in the activity.

Each of us has the capacity for various types of engagement, but the interests and concerns which make it possible to involve ourselves fully in an activity often need cultivation. Although some activities seem to capture our attention spontaneously with little effort, many of the most satisfying kinds of involvement require us to prepare ourselves through disciplined practice and training. Sometimes it is only by an extended process that we develop a taste for a particular type of engagement and allow an incipient interest to become an absorbing passion.

As we cultivate the capacities for particular types of engagement, we give shape to the self. Giving the self a particular shape is both to expand its possibilities and to limit them. A person who has developed the capacity for a deep understanding of politics may find that some ways of thinking she had before beginning the study have become so alien as to be barely conceivable. A man who has become passionately concerned about social justice may discover it next to impossible to let a prejudiced remark pass unchallenged in the name of preserving comfortable social interactions.

If we try to keep all our options open by refraining from forming any deep concerns or interests, we are by this strategy closing off those engagements which require deep and abiding commitments. One does not become obsessed with physics or absorbed in community service or even passionately consumed by love for another person without shaping the self in ways that cannot be altered at will. Seeking only those kinds of engagements that leave the self utterly free means seeking a life in which some of the satisfactions humans have found preeminently fulfilling must be relinquished.

An extreme form of holding back from any engagements that might entangle the self is to try to make the pursuit of self-interest one's only concern. If one aspires to be the kind of person who cares only about his own benefit, then it is necessary to establish a tight rein over any inclination that might pull in some other direction. So concern for other people must be kept at a fairly superficial level, as must concern for goals like improving the school system or creating a beautiful work of art. If concerns such as these are allowed to find a deep residence within the self, then they can potentially challenge the exclusive concern with getting benefits for the self. The only concerns that can be permitted are those that can easily be turned off when the reflective self judges them to conflict with paths offering greater benefits.

However, developing only shallow concerns that one can take or leave means giving up the possibility of many kinds of engagements. If I care only a little about scientific truth, I will not be able to be deeply absorbed in scientific work. If my love of beauty is so much on the surface that I can turn it on or off, my capacity for experiencing the beauty of art or nature will be very limited. If my interest in another person remains casual, I have no chance at experiencing the satisfactions of a deeply personal relationship with that person. If I think these kinds of engagements are crucial to the kind of life I want to have, building a self concerned only about its own interest will be a self-defeating strategy for me.

From the perspective of a self concerned only about its own benefit, the prospect of being motivated by other concerns seems risky. It might involve becoming a person who cares so much about some goal outside the self that she is willing to sacrifice things that currently seem crucial to her well-being. However, the refusal to develop any deep concerns is also a risky strategy. It means giving up the possibility of engagements that might have proved deeply satisfying and fulfilling. Ultimately each of us needs to decide what kinds of engagement are crucial to the sort of life we want to have and to accept whatever risk is involved in building the kind of self who is capable of living that life. There is no risk-free alternative.

Part Three

BECOMING A SELF

I can't explain *myself*, I'm afraid, Sir...because I'm not myself, you see. (Alice in Lewis Carroll's *Alice's Adventures in Wonderland*[1])

The self the individual knows is simultaneously the actual self and the ideal self, which the individual has outside himself as the image in whose likeness he is to form himself, and which on the other hand he has within himself, since it is he himself. (Judge Wilhelm in Kierkegaard's *Either/Or*[2])

PRELUDE TO PART THREE

To be a self is to have a unified orientation by means of which you order your life. Developing and applying the orientation to your activities is a process which in different individuals is achieved with varying degrees of success. Hence, an individual may be on the way to becoming a self, or one might have a fragmented existence in which genuine selfhood is a remote prospect.

Chapter Nine discusses what it means to have an identity. In contrast to a life which responds to the pressures of the moment without any stable structure or a life of chaotic impulses, an individual may define herself by means of a relatively lasting set of beliefs and values that provide a unified orientation. However, the orientation one claims and identifies with needs to be brought into harmony with the individual's actual engagements. Failure to do so means a kind of disintegration of the self and a life without firm convictions or enduring commitments.

The self with a strong identity will have to operate within limits, but the limits reflect what that self cares about. To desire a life in which all options are open means desiring a self without any deep concerns. But a self without deep concerns will be incapable of many ways of life that reflective individuals find most attractive. In seeking to express the concerns that constitute our identity, we must find patterns of social expression that allow us to put them into practice. Although social forms can restrict an identity, they can also furnish the means for giving it concrete expression.

An identity that integrates moral concerns into the self blurs the lines between morality and self-interest that exist in some people's experience. For a person with this sort of integration, moral actions are essential expressions of the self. Although such a person may still face conflicts, the conflicts are of a different nature from those of an individual who has failed to integrate her moral concerns into her identity.

Chapter Ten addresses the issue of maintaining an identity. When we stand for something, there may be a personal price to be paid. The virtue that enables us to hold ourselves together and resist pressures to compromise our fundamental convictions is called integrity. The person of integrity has limits. There are things that she cannot do without betraying her self, and maintaining these limits is necessary to maintaining a self this person can respect.

The exercise of integrity involves a willingness to suffer ill consequences of maintaining identity-defining convictions. In some cases exercising integrity can mean significant suffering or even death. From one perspective the person of integrity will sometimes be acting against self-interest. However, individuals with integrity are likely to see a concern with protecting the self as overriding all other interests. Protecting the self requires not only withstanding pressures, but also avoiding patterns of self-deception which can support a fragmentation of identity.

Chapter Eleven makes clear why achieving and maintaining an identity is a project in self-transformation. To live the life we want, we need to bring our various impulses into harmony with the reflective orientation we identify with. We mold what we become by the way we act. Our actions establish the traits and the habitual patterns that may support or conflict with our chosen way of life. However, we are also formed by what we love and admire. As we cultivate appreciation of the ideals which help to define our identity, we give ourselves a powerful motivation to live in accordance with those ideals. While our efforts do not guarantee happiness, they may be necessary for the kind of life that a reflective person would be willing to call happy.

Chapter Nine

IDENTITY

Our identity is what allows us to define what is important to us and what is not. (Charles Taylor[1])

...if a man were always anxious that he himself above all things, should act justly, temperately, or in accordance with any other of the virtues, and in general were always to try to secure for himself the honourable course, no one will call such a man a lover of self or blame him. (Aristotle[2])

If, therefore, I am where my moral purpose is, then, and then only, will I be the friend and son and the father that I should be. For then this will be my interest—to keep my good faith, my self-respect, my forbearance, my abstinence, and my cooperation, and to maintain my relations with other men. (Epictetus[3])

At some point in your life someone is likely to advise you, "Be yourself." On one level this advice seems remarkably inane. What else could you be other than yourself? Typically, however, the advice comes when self-consciousness has tied you up in knots or when you are tempted to pretend to be more sophisticated or well-informed than you really are. In such a context the advice often amounts to a suggestion that you relax and put aside any efforts to impress anyone. Instead, let your habitual patterns of thought and action take charge.

While such advice is sometimes appropriate, it should not pass unnoticed that its value depends on whether you have developed a self that is adequate to deal with the situation you are facing. It is entirely possible that when you relax and put aside any pretense, the self that is revealed may lack the qualities that will evoke a positive response in others. Or when you show people what you are really like, it may become perfectly obvious that you are incompetent in some area where you were supposed to be skillful. Trying to be yourself works best when you are appropriately confident about the self you have.

Of course, that is the rub. It is usually when you are insecure about the self you have that you are tempted to adopt a pretense. The false front is a way of hiding from others, and perhaps from yourself, what you might be ashamed of. If you had enough self-confidence to begin with, it would scarcely be necessary to remind you to be yourself. But acquiring self-confidence ordinarily means following a long-term strategy for becoming the kind of self who can be revealed to others without embarrassment or regret. Failure to develop such a self can make pretense very inviting.

THE LOSS OF IDENTITY

The film, *Zelig*[4], portrays in pseudo-documentary style the life of the fictional character, Leonard Zelig. In the 1920s and 30s Zelig rises to public prominence because of a remarkable ability. He becomes like the people he is with. When he is with Boston socialites, he speaks in a Bostonian accent and adopts the style of a socialite, espousing Republican ideas that are sure to be well-received by that group. When he is with members of the working class, he takes on their characteristic language and mannerisms, advocating Democratic ideas and candidates. For Zelig these displays are not a matter of hypocrisy. In each encounter he undergoes a transformation to think like and act like the people he happens to be near.

In the film Zelig's transformations are portrayed as including physical as well as psychological changes. When he is among a group of Rabbis, he quickly grows a long beard as he begins to engage in theological discussion. When he is among Orientals, he acquires Oriental features. When he is with blacks, his skin turns black. Whatever characteristics will enable him to blend in, magically appear, allowing Zelig to be swallowed up by the role of the moment.

This abnormality is treated by a psychiatrist who discovers

that Zelig's condition arose out of a childhood desire to be safe and secure. As a protective mechanism, he attempted to find security by being like other people to gain their acceptance. On a small scale this behavior started when he pretended to have read books he had not read to fit in with the brighter students in school. Eventually the desperate urge to blend resulted in habitual transformations beyond his control. In the popular media Zelig is labeled a human chameleon, for his protective strategy resembles that of the lizard who changes colors to blend in with its environment.

Zelig's transformations are so total that he becomes whatever role he is playing. In one sense he displays a remarkable strength: the ability to sense the environment completely and to change himself to fit it. But this strength is at the same time a fatal flaw. His infinite flexibility is purchased at the price of a loss of his own identity. Zelig has no secure sense of who he is. If he is among doctors, he assumes the mannerisms and thought processes of a doctor, and he actually believes that he is a doctor. The roles he plays come to dominate him so much that his life becomes a series of roles with no stable self beyond them.

While Zelig is a fictional character, his story can reveal some disconcerting features of our own situation. To some extent we are all like Zelig, seeking to win the approval of others. Our ability to fit in by absorbing social expectations allows us to adjust ourselves in ways that produce comfortable interactions. However, the price of comfort can be significant pressures on the self. We may not disappear into our social personas, but our conformity to perceived social demands is often at cross purposes with our efforts to maintain a unified identity.

As William James puts it, a person

> has as many different social selves as there are distinct *groups* of persons about whose opinion he cares. He generally shows a different side of himself to each of these different groups. Many a youth who is demure enough before his parents and teachers, swears and swaggers like a pirate among his 'tough' young friends. We do not show ourselves to our children as to our club companions, to our customers as to

> the laborers we employ, to our own masters and employees as to our intimate friends. From this there results what practically is a division of man into several selves....[5]

It is easy to assume that amidst all this diversity is a unified self, unaffected by the demands of social reality. However, some of our performances are difficult to combine with our sense of who we really are, and when the values we display in our actions are at odds with the values we claim to be ours, it is reasonable to wonder whether the self we assume remains intact. While we are not in danger of losing the self to the extent that Zelig did, it may take some effort to respond to the various pressures of our social situation in a way that preserves whatever we take to be crucial to our identity. Without this effort, the self we retain may turn out to be different from any self we could recognize or affirm.

HAVING AN IDENTITY

Suppose that we imagine an individual to be merely a bundle of distinct impulses to act. Such an individual would not yet be what we call a person or a self, for a person must be capable of choice, and choosing presupposes a distinction between the agent and her impulses. One who makes choices may endorse certain impulses and reject others, but that requires the capacity for getting a critical distance from the impulses sufficient for evaluating them. Someone who was indistinguishable from her impulses would not be in control of them.

Becoming a self calls for forming an evaluative perspective sufficient for determining which impulses to claim as one's own and which to resist. Through developing a system of beliefs, values, and commitments, an individual is able to organize the potentially chaotic realm of impulses and establish priorities among them. This organizing structure enables one to develop an orientation that provides a unified basis for action. By identifying with this relatively stable orientation, one forms a self capable of exercising a degree of control over its destiny.

It is by the process of actually exercising (and failing to exercise) control that an individual establishes an identity. By adopting the evaluative perspective produced by a set of beliefs, values, and commitments, a person can potentially shape her desires and actions into a relatively coherent whole. To the extent that one is successful in doing this, she has developed an identity or a unified self.

The term "identity" is used in a variety of ways. My use corresponds, I believe, to the sense in which people speak of having an identity crisis. One experiencing such a crisis loses hold on the stable structure of meanings which makes possible a unified self, becoming disoriented and confused. A person facing an identity crisis is puzzled about such issues as, "What do I really believe?" "What do I care about?" "What can I regard as genuinely worth doing?" "What am I willing to commit myself to?"

In a different kind of society these questions might have had less urgency. When society is homogeneous with regard to a fundamental framework of beliefs and when social roles are fairly rigidly assigned, individuals have no great need to come up with their own beliefs and values or to try to find their place. However, in a pluralistic society without a clear authority structure an individual may need to weigh various belief options in deciding how to live. Furthermore, when a society allows a significant range of freedom, a person is faced with many possible ways of ordering a life.

Sometimes people in our context speak of the search for identity as a matter of "finding oneself." This metaphor is somewhat misleading if it suggests searching until I come upon an already-formed object. Even if a person could "look inside" to discover something, how would she know that the object discovered was *her* identity? The quest for identity undoubtedly requires elements of discovery, but the task is more fundamentally a matter of defining oneself or choosing oneself where the definition or choice is not determined in advance. I find myself when I am able to formulate the stable structure of beliefs and values that I will live by.

The self to be defined is one that I am willing to call my own. The structure furnished by a set of beliefs, values, and commitments can only provide a unified orientation for one who identifies with the evaluative perspective it produces. Only when I acknowledge the viewpoint resulting from a set of beliefs as *my* viewpoint and the concerns underlying the values I formulate as *my* concerns can those beliefs and values give me a frame of reference sufficient to distinguish the self from its impulses. The beliefs, values, and commitments that allow me to develop an identity cannot be put on or taken off like a suit of clothes, for the orientation they provide me is only possible when what I am is inseparable from what I believe and what I care about.

One of the peculiarities of the hypothetical case of Zelig is that the unified orientation we expect of a person is missing. If we ask what Zelig really believes or what he really cares about, we are at a loss, for his surrender to the impulse to fit in has displaced any stable features needed for an identity. His habitual conformity to the beliefs and concerns of others has taken the place of whatever self he might have called his own.

Unlike Zelig all of us are confident that we can distinguish between the real self and the various selves revealed in our social performances. However, making this distinction is not as easy as it might seem. Our efforts to say what we really believe or care about are subject to many forms of self-deception and confusion. Furthermore, there are likely to be areas where the self is incompletely formed. When you try to determine what you believe or value, there may be no answer in these areas until you are pressed to work out a definite stance. Given these difficulties, knowing who you are is unlikely to be an instantaneous achievement, and people will experience varying degrees of success when they try to say what they hold to be fundamentally important or valuable, what basic convictions shape their character, and what commitments govern their understanding of life's options.

It might seem surprising that anyone would have to struggle to define her convictions. Don't we all know what we believe? Isn't it obvious what we take to be important? Often the answer is no. Sometimes we repeat empty formulas we have heard from others, assuming that they must express our belief too. But when these "beliefs" have little to do with how we live or how we interpret our experience, they are apt to become superfluous. In thinking about our identity we are sometimes attempting to discover what beliefs do (or could) give coherent order to our behavior and make sense of our experience. The formulas we assume to express what we stand for may need to be replaced by something that does greater justice to our reality.

Similarly, the values we might think to be ours may have little connection with the way we actually live. Unless we can give our values a motivating force, we cannot really claim them as our own. Reflection on who you are is sometimes a matter of determining what values are indispensable components of a self you would be willing to accept and judging whether you can transform your current self to incorporate these values. Hence, discovering one's identity is not merely a matter of empirical observation; it includes formulating aspirations and measuring them against an assessment of the possibilities. If I identify with certain aspirations, they become crucial to my project of defining who I am.

An identity in the sense I am using the term is an achievement. However, the extent to which one develops a stable structure that can provide a unified orientation will be a matter of degree. Building a strong identity means laying claim to your actions in a way that produces a fundamental harmony between them and the beliefs and values that you reflectively acknowledge as your own. Obviously, not everyone achieves this kind of harmony. Should the prospect of having a relatively weak identity be a matter of concern? Would a person who lacks the kind of integration a strong identity offers miss anything important?

Consider the extreme form of disintegration exhibited by Zelig. What is it about Zelig that strikes us as undesirable? One way to approach this question is to consider the kind of trade-off Zelig makes. He treats the value of fitting in as preeminent, something important enough to give up every other value to achieve. If he has fundamental convictions of his own, he will get rid of them so he can conform his beliefs to those he is around. If he cares deeply about any goals other than fitting in, he will drop those concerns. If he has commitments to anything, he will alter them to adopt temporarily the commitments of those he is with.

Is this a good bargain? The only kind of person who could answer yes would be someone who lacked deep convictions, who did not really care about anything other than fitting in, and who had no firm commitments—in other words, someone who completely lacked an identity. To a person who has an identity that is shaped by these things, the prospect of giving them up amounts to a destruction of the self that is analogous to dying. Anyone who has firm convictions or deep commitments ought to be able to see why the trade-off is wildly incommensurate with any expected gains.

Furthermore, the prospect of being someone like Zelig should strike most people as horrifying. Take, for example, Zelig's lack of firm beliefs or convictions. Zelig's opinions are a function of the role he is playing at the moment. At one point in the film, Zelig falls in with a group of Nazis in 1930s Germany, enthusiastically supporting ideas conducive to producing a master race. He fits in as easily with Hitler's followers as he does with any other group.

The question of whether developing a strong identity is desirable hinges on the issue of how important it is to establish control over your own life. To have a relatively weak identity is to be at the mercy of impulses which the self has not made its own. It is also to refuse to give unqualified affirmation to whatever beliefs and values you claim. You can try to live without any firm convictions, but it is unlikely that your reflective self will be able to maintain the kind of neutrality this stance requires. In practical terms you will make some judgments about what is true and what is valuable, and a refusal to allow these judgments to shape you amounts to a refusal to take your own judgments seriously. Hence, failing to develop a strong identity involves a rejection or suppression of a fundamental part of the self.

By contrast, to have a strong identity is to possess a relatively stable center of gravity that can help you to find your way amidst the various pressures that could lead you to deny your values or violate your convictions. One who possesses such an identity will find that some actions are ruled out in advance and others are obviously called for. Hence, having a strong identity sometimes replaces the need for extended reflection or even decision, since some actions clearly express the fundamental orientation which constitutes the self. For example, in much of the social science research about people who perform heroic actions to help others, the actors did not think about what they were doing as heroic. They simply did what needed to be done. It was not a matter of deciding to act. Given the beliefs and values that constituted their way of seeing the world, they were not aware of an alternative.

IDENTITY AND FREEDOM

Having an identity limits one's options. If my identity is structured by a deep concern for another person, acting in ways that hurt that person may be difficult or impossible for me. If I have identified myself with certain religious beliefs, I may find that I cannot repudiate these beliefs even under threat of torture or death. In other words, having an identity means that I will have a psychological makeup that prevents me from considering some choices as options for me.

Some people will see this as a significant limitation on freedom. Their picture of freedom includes the idea of keeping your options open. If you are limited by your psychological structure in a way that takes some options off the table or makes them excessively difficult, then in this view you are not fully free.

However, the kind of freedom imagined here is the freedom of someone who lacks any deep concerns. That person is free to do anything only because nothing matters much to such a person. But an individual to whom nothing matters much can hardly exhibit the kind of freedom we should value. Harry Frankfurt explains why:

> A person's ideals are concerns that he cannot bring himself to betray. They entail constraints that, for him, it is unthinkable to violate. Suppose that someone has no ideals at all. In that case, nothing is unthinkable for him; there are no limits to what he might be willing to do. He can make whatever decisions he likes and shape his will just as he pleases. This does not mean that his will is free. It means only that his will is anarchic, moved by mere impulse and inclination.[6]

Making free choices requires an identity with enough substance to give direction to a will that you can claim as your own.

Perhaps, however, the objection is not to all kinds of identity, but only those that involve deep convictions or ultimate commitments that could tie one's hands too much. As a suggestion about how to increase freedom, this idea is paradoxical. For what it rules out is the option of becoming a person who cares deeply about some things and is strongly committed to pursuing a particular way of living. People whose identities are formed by deep and overpowering concerns of this kind often report that the experience of acting out of these concerns generates an intense feeling of freedom. In fact, people hardly ever feel as free as when they are bound by love. One who wants to reject this option is in the name of freedom is ruling out the freedom to adopt a way of life that might be intensely fulfilling.

A related problem is that the desire to keep all one's options open may itself express a kind of ultimate identity-shaping concern, the concern to maximize personal advantage. One whose identity is formed by an overriding concern with personal advantage can try to mold a self that is able to consider all the options in a given situation that he thinks will lead to this end, but as previous chapters show, it is far from clear that being this kind of self is conducive to having a satisfying life. So seeking to keep one's options open comes at a cost: giving up the sort of self-formation needed for many attractive ways of living. When we think about the issue of what kind of life one might attain, it looks as if the most important freedom is the freedom to become the self one aspires to be, even if that self will not have unlimited options.

What limits the options of a self with a particular identity are the concerns an individual has incorporated into that self. But these limitations are simply the other side of the coin to being able to express a self which cares about some things. Being relieved of these limitations means emptying the self of much of the substance that makes certain kinds of meaningful and satisfying ways of living possible.

EXPRESSING ONE'S IDENTITY

Developing an identity is a long-term project, and a crucial part of that project is finding ways to express the fundamental concerns that an individual claims as her own. Earlier I suggested that there can be social pressures that compromise our efforts to produce a unified self, but it would be one-sided to see this as the whole story. Social forms also furnish us with opportunities for developing and giving expression to the self. It is through adopting particular roles and participating in social institutions that a person gives concrete form to identity-shaping values.

For example, by participating in a social institution such as marriage one forms the self in accordance with the values that are built into the institution and the roles it contains. To become a husband or a wife is not just to play a role. It is to take into the self certain commitments and ideals that give a definitive shape to one's identity. One of the reasons that divorce is a traumatic event for most people is that it forces a person to redefine an identity from which key elements have been removed. Similarly, a social role such as mother will have expectations and ideals which a woman takes as her own. Her identification with the norms of this role can become vital to her sense of achievement and self-worth.

In our society one of the most important identity-shaping choices a person faces is the choice of vocation. Although some people think of their work life only in terms of time they have to put in in order to live their real lives, most people invest themselves in varying degrees in their work. Being able to think about what you do for a living as worthwhile and being able to think that you are doing a good job are undoubtedly key elements in job satisfaction. When one can get a sense of personal accomplishment from work, it also adds greatly to life satisfaction. Conversely failure at work or unemployment can be significant blows to a person's self-esteem. If I identify strongly with my job as a teacher, it will not be easy to acknowledge that I am a poor teacher.

A job can have significant formative effects on the way we think and on what we notice. In fact, those jobs that we call professions involve training that molds an individual's thinking and perception in prescribed directions. One learns to think like a lawyer or an engineer, asking the right kinds of questions and organizing the data at hand in accordance with the concepts and rules of the profession. This kind of formation is not something that one can sharply separate from her identity. Learning the skills and values of a profession is likely to affect areas of life outside of work. Think, for example, of the counselor who cannot drop out of the counseling mode, even during casual social interactions.

Given the potential effects on identity of work life, it is important to consider how well a particular line of work will allow an individual to express her identity. Unfortunately, people often fail to take this into consideration. On several occasions I have asked a class of business students, "What if you were offered a high-paying job in the tobacco industry? Would you have any reservations about taking it?" Very few students have said that they would have any problem at all. When I included the phrase "high-paying," that was all they needed to hear. Students typically comment that as long as the work they were offered was legal, they would have no qualms about doing it.

In these discussions students never brought up ideas such as, "Would I be willing to devote a considerable amount of my time and ability to making a product that is known to be harmful to people's health?" or "Would the work allow me to contribute to society in any meaningful way?" No one ever asked, "What would I be like after doing this kind of work for ten or fifteen years?" Instead they focused on the question of whether the work would violate any obligation, usually concluding that it would not because the customers were not coerced into buying the product, but chose to do so.

When we think about vocational options, it is easy to overlook the ways that they are likely to form our identity, for good or ill. It is possible to do the kind of work in the kind of organization that will contribute to your development toward being the sort of person you want to be. But it is also possible to devote yourself to work in an organization that stifles your ideals and channels your energy in directions that enhance your cynicism and narrow your range of interests. We do not form an identity in isolation, but in community, and when we take a clear-headed look, we can often have some advance awareness of whether the associations and the institutional roles we invest ourselves in will take us closer to or farther from being the persons we want to be.

IDENTITY AND SELF-LOVE

The ancient philosopher, Aristotle, raises in his *Nicomachean Ethics* the question of whether self-love is a good or a bad thing. His answer is that there are different meanings to the phrase "lover of self." Some people use this phrase to refer to people who are concerned primarily with gratifying their appetites or what Aristotle calls the "irrational element of the soul." Those who are lovers of self in this sense are concerned to gain for themselves "the greater share of wealth, honours, and bodily pleasure ..."[7] They treat their own interest in these things as more important than other people's interest and, hence, focus on satisfying it, even if it is at the expense of others. Aristotle claims that this kind of lover of self may be justifiably reproached, and he asserts that most people are like this.

However, there is another way to use the phrase "lover of self." What if a person "assigns to himself the things that are noblest and best, and gratifies the most authoritative element in himself and in all things obeys this ..."[8] Or, to use the language developed earlier in this chapter, what if a person identifies himself, not with the impulses he happens to have, but with the evaluative perspective by which he organizes those impulses? For such a person being a lover of self would mean having ideals for the self which incorporate what he judges most valuable and admirable. It would mean claiming impulses insofar as they fit in to his overall conception of the kind of person he aspires to be. If we use the term in this way, however, it need not be a term of derision or criticism, for one who loves worthy ideals will be acting in a fashion deserving of praise and approval. So Aristotle concludes, "Therefore the good man should be a lover of self (for he will both himself profit by doing noble acts, and will benefit his fellows), but the wicked man should not; for he will hurt both himself and his neighbours, following as he does evil passions."[9]

Aristotle's vision of ideal development involves an identification between the self and its considered judgments of what things are valuable and worthy of admiration. While recognizing that there are impulses that could pull one toward a way of life that fails to match up with this reflective valuation, he pictures the admirable person as having achieved a kind of integration in which action will habitually express a self formed in accordance with certain ideals of human excellence. When one loves and identifies with this kind of self, the potential conflict between selfish behavior and moral behavior is transformed.

Aristotle is optimistic that the proper use of reason will lead us to good principles. Even if we are less optimistic, we can acknowledge that his vision of ideal development can help us to understand how motivations that we call moral can be powerfully integrated into a person's life. For some people, what is morally right is sharply distinguishable from what is personally advantageous. It is as if there are separate systems which are not well connected. However, for others the lines between moral beliefs and personal goals are not sharply drawn. Their personal identity is one which is partially constituted by moral concerns. For one who has unified the self in this way there is a strong motivation to act in ways that are consistent with the core identity.

In a series of studies of individuals who were designated by others as moral exemplars, psychologists Colby and Damon concluded that their subjects had integrated their sense of self with morality to a higher degree than most people. They write, "Rather than denying the self, they define it with a moral center. They seamlessly integrate their commitments with their personal concerns, so that the fulfillment of one implies the fulfillment of the other."[10] These authors argue that although the subjects of their study were exceptional, the kind of development they exhibited could be recognized as similar to the process of self-formation and moral development in any normal human life. Virtually everyone takes on some moral commitments which become defining components of the self. However, the moral exemplars achieved an unusual degree of integration that gave strong support to their natural moral inclinations.

For a person whose moral concerns are woven into her sense of self, there is no sharp division between doing what is morally right and pursuing self-interest. Colby and Damon say that their exemplars started "from the assumption that their own interests were synonymous with their moral goals."[11] In pursuing their projects of social justice or aiding more vulnerable members of society, they were expressing a self that was profoundly invested in achieving these goals. The conflict they faced was not between morality and self-interest but of deciding how best to use their limited time and energy.

Most of us do not have such a well-integrated identity. We have moral principles and ideals that we claim as our own, but we also have individual goals and concerns that can potentially conflict with our moral aspirations. While most of the time we can allow these two systems to have a relatively conflict-free existence, there are times when we are strongly tempted to lie, cheat, or steal or otherwise compromise our moral selves. To a large extent the conflicts we face reflect a failure to establish a unified identity. We are divided selves who have not committed ourselves to a priority structure that clearly defines who we are.

Though we might think that we can sit on the fence, we ultimately define ourselves by our action. Whether we realize it or not, when we give in to temptations to compromise our moral principles or act to uphold them, we are, in effect, declaring how important they will be to us and how significant a role they will play in establishing our identity. However, the definition we give ourselves through action may or may not coincide with the identity we would have chosen to have. In a particular instance of struggle between elements of a divided self, it may not seem that much is at stake. Only rarely do we realize that we are confronted with an identity-constituting choice.

We sometimes view such struggles as conflicts between morality and self-interest. But whether this is an appropriate way of thinking depends on the kind of self one aspires to have. If the self whose interests are to be promoted is conceived as an essentially moral self, then its interests lie in acting in a way that helps to produce and maintain an integrated moral identity. The Roman Emperor Marcus Aurelius must have been thinking along this line when he wrote,

> Never esteem as beneficial to yourself what will compel you to break faith, to abandon self-respect, to hate, suspect, or curse anyone, to dissemble.... A man who has chosen the side of mind and spirit within him...should not adopt a way of life alien to a thinker and social being..."[12]

Having an identity seems like the easiest thing in the world, but having an identity that is unified in the way you want it to be is a challenging task. Kierkegaard conceives of the matter in a helpful way. When you see the need for choosing a self, you will become aware of a kind of ideal self that could give you the sort of unified identity you aspire to. While this ideal is not yet your identity, it is not something alien either, for the ideal represents your own awareness of how you may become a single self, rather than a fragmented bundle. In working to match your aspirations with the reality of your life, you are striving to become yourself.

Chapter Ten

INTEGRITY

Generally speaking, with the emergence of the person in the individual, there is a tendency for increasing correlation between what is avowed by the person and the actual engagements of the individual. It is in terms of the tacit ideal of perfect harmony in this respect that we tend to assess the individual. (Herbert Fingarette[1])

Without integrity and the identity-conferring commitments it assumes, there would be nothing to fear the loss of, not because we are safe but because we have nothing to lose. (Lynn McFall[2])

There are occasions when a person realizes that what he cares about matters to him not merely so much, but in such a way, that it is impossible for him to forbear from a certain course of action. (Harry Frankfurt[3])

The price of developing and maintaining an identity may not be cheap. Moreover, we are not generally in a position to estimate in advance how great it will be. When we form ourselves in accordance with particular values and commitments, we don't yet know what specific actions will be required of us. Often the implications of a particular kind of self-formation are only gradually apparent, and sometimes circumstances conspire to put the partially-formed self to the test.

Andrei Sakharov, inventor of the Soviet hydrogen bomb, was the youngest person ever elected to the Academy of Sciences of the Soviet Union.[4] A brilliant physicist, he was a member of the privileged class in Soviet society. Until age thirty-six he devoted himself to a distinguished scientific career, enjoying the honors and rewards that went with his achievements. Then his life began to take a turn that no one reviewing the early evidence could have predicted.

In 1957 Sakharov became concerned over radioactivity produced by nuclear weapons tests. He circulated memos to his fellow scientists to alert them to the problem and to urge them to exercise caution. In 1961 he met with Premier Kruschev to urge him to halt nuclear tests. Kruschev's response was that he should return to his own work and cease meddling in the affairs of state. In 1966 Sakharov sent an open letter to the Soviet congress in which he warned against the prospect of a new Stalinism. The next year he wrote to Brezhnev, protesting harsh sentences of two Soviet dissidents.

In 1968 Sakharov allowed writings in which he argued for détente to be published in the West. As a result he lost his clearance for scientific work and his government job. In the next few years Sakharov, along with other intellectuals, formed the Moscow Human Rights Committee. Started as a discussion group, the organization eventually became an advocate for victims of government persecution throughout the Soviet Union.

By 1973 Sakharov was appealing for help from international agencies for Soviet citizens being held in psychiatric hospitals. He was officially warned not to talk to foreigners. In the next few years Sakharov was attacked in the Soviet media and eventually exiled from Moscow to Gorki. After 1987, under Gorbachev, he was allowed to return from exile. By the time of his death he was widely known and appreciated throughout the Soviet Union as a man of integrity.

Sakharov's story is a striking example of a self in the process of development. At one point his identity is structured around his scientific work. But gradually as he became aware of various social issues, the values he implicitly acknowledged seemed to call for specific action. He did not set out to challenge the Soviet system, but his persistence put him into conflict with the official power structure. At numerous points he had the opportunity to pull back and lessen the risk to himself, but Sakharov increasingly identified with his moral concerns, putting himself on the line to take a stand against wrongs that came to his attention.

Colby and Damon evaluate his involvement as follows: "For Sakharov, the values of truth and justice were so central to his personal identity that he could not allow himself to draw back from the challenges he encountered regardless of the conflicts and the risks they presented."[5] While we can, in retrospect, discern fundamental values in Sakharov's identity, the self that gradually emerges is made possible by his willingness to see the implications of taking these values as important and acting on them. Though he was inclined to exercise restraint, his awareness of conditions pressed him toward a recognition that he must do what he could.

Sakharov could have drawn back. He could, as others did, have rationalized inaction in an authoritarian and oppressive society. However, his initial steps turned into a tenacious commitment. Exhibiting a remarkable receptiveness to having his perspective enlarged by others, Sakharov pursued his goals in a way that resulted in an admirable integration of the self. He achieved this integration by continually acting as if the values he identified with really mattered.

BEING TRUE TO YOURSELF

Many of my beliefs have no firm connection with my identity. I believe that Austin is the capital of Texas, but if strong evidence convinced me that this belief was wrong, it would make little difference for the conduct of my life. However, some of my beliefs are so tied to my understanding of what is real or what is important that to alter them would mean a radical upheaval. If I have built a life around working for the inevitable triumph of Marx's communist society, and world events convince me that my lifework is futile, I may undergo a crisis of identity in which I attempt to redefine what I believe (and who I am).

Beliefs that are fundamental to an individual's identity may be called convictions. Because convictions are deeply embedded in a person's patterns of understanding, the implications of giving them up are far-reaching. Consider, for example, Suzie Valdez's belief in God (Chapter Eight). This belief plays a crucial role in how she understands the events of her life. She sees reality as an arena in which God calls people to particular tasks and gives them the resources they need to do the assigned job. To eliminate this belief would mean tearing down the whole structure of meanings by which she makes sense of her experiences. Giving it up would require a radical change in her sense of who she is.

Since convictions are so closely tied to the self, failing to live by them or stand up for them can seem like a betrayal of the self. Suppose that you are in business and your best customer asks you for a contribution to a political cause that you regard as despicable. You have intentionally avoided discussing politics with this customer because of an intuition that it might be a source of conflict. However, the customer assumes that you must think as he does. The contribution is small enough that from a business point of view it would be well worth the expense to keep in the customer's good graces, but giving the money would mean failing to stand up for something you regard as vitally important. The idea of keeping quiet and signing a check leaves a bad taste in your mouth, for meeting the concerns of your business self comes perilously close to a betrayal of your fundamental identity. You might be able to rationalize it, but if you have any sensitivity, you will not be able to regard it as trivial or inconsequential.

The virtue at stake here is what we usually call integrity. The etymological meaning of this term is wholeness or unity. The underlying idea is that a person will have some fundamental convictions or basic principles by which she defines herself. Acting in ways that are consistent with holding these principles allows an individual to keep her identity intact. However, acting as if identity-defining convictions were unimportant weakens their hold and risks a kind of fragmentation of identity. One who acts with integrity does what is needed for holding the self together.

Of course, whether we apply this term to a particular individual may depend on whether the identity-defining convictions are ones we approve of. A Mafia leader whose code included killing anyone who was a threat to the organization might be maintaining a unitary character by ordering a hit, but if we think that character is despicable, we will probably not refer to this leader as a person of integrity.

Nevertheless, we can sometimes recognize and admire an individual's integrity even when we don't agree with the underlying convictions. What we admire in such cases is a willingness to stand up for one's beliefs even when circumstances make this difficult. The virtue of integrity is about holding onto your fundamental convictions rather than giving in to the pressure of the moment.

If we were never pressured to compromise our convictions, we would not need the kind of character strength we call integrity. But realistically anyone with firm principles or commitments will find that there are times when it would be much easier to ignore them. Being honest may give me a sense of satisfaction, but there are times when a deviation from honesty offers very tempting tangible benefits. Being a person of integrity means living by convictions even when the payoff structure is rigged in the other direction.

Often we can say that it is in a person's interest to maintain her identity even when the potential loss from doing so is great. One reason for this is that the loss of integrity does not quite fit on the same scale as other potential gains or losses. Suppose I have the opportunity to make a great deal of money, but to do so I must violate a deeply held conviction or commitment. How much money would such a violation be worth? Some people believe that every person has his price. If you make the potential benefits great enough, they hold, there is no one who will not at some point sell out. But even if this were true, there is something puzzling about the judgment that one's integrity is worth $50,000 or $50,000,000. It is not puzzling that one might be tempted or might yield to the temptation. What is puzzling is how something which is crucial to my identity could be worth any amount of money.

Money is valuable insofar as it can provide benefits for some self, but if some act will destroy my identity, the benefits it can afford will not be for my self, but for another. That is, if acting in some way goes against my evaluative perspective to the extent that it amounts to a repudiation of that perspective, I do not remain the person I was. I either develop a new evaluative perspective, or I disintegrate as a person. But the evaluative perspective I have now represents what is important to me, and to repudiate what is important to me is to give up on my whole way of life. Whatever might replace my best-considered judgments of what is worthwhile cannot be something I am now able to accept and identify with. So the cost of sacrificing my identity is to give up the kind of life I am reflectively able to choose for myself.

Voluntarily choosing to compromise integrity also means a loss of self-respect. As Gabriele Taylor puts it,

> A person can have self-respect, or a sense of her own value, only if she believes some form of life is worth living and believes that by and large she is capable of leading such a life. Self-respect must be based on what she takes to be her commitments, for it must be based on that in virtue of which she thinks herself worthy of respect...to have self-respect she must have a degree of integrity; without some integrity there would be no self to respect.[6]

In the loss of integrity there are two dangers, both of which are fearful. One is becoming the kind of person I despise. The other is losing the orienting perspective that allows me both to exercise judgment about myself and control over my life.

Of course, when a person does compromise a conviction, she does not typically perceive this as an identity-changing event. We find it easy to convince ourselves that we can be a little dishonest without becoming dishonest persons, or somewhat deceptive without being liars, or even that we can habitually act in ways contrary to our religious beliefs without being hypocrites. But what this amounts to is a failure to hold convictions in a way that could give us an identity. Our willingness to give in when the pressures or the incentives are great enough indicates the absence of convictions or commitments that go deep into the self.

There is an old story that George Bernard Shaw, while seated next to a young woman at a dinner party, attempted to engage her in a serious conversation. The issue raised was about how much it might take for people to do something that they would find repugnant. Shaw asked the young woman, "Would you sleep with me for one-million pounds?" After a little thought, she said that for that much money, she would. "Then," asked Shaw, "Would you sleep with me for one pound?" Insulted, the woman asked with indignation, "What do you take me for?" Shaw's response was, "We have already established that. Now we're just haggling over the price."

Like it or not, what we are willing to do says something about what we are. It can make an odious self-description unavoidable, or it can make a self-description to which we attach great importance impossible. Being willing to betray a friend for the sake of career advancement says much about the kind of friend I am. Being willing to use my marketing talents to promote cigarette smoking among teenagers reveals the hollowness of my claims to care about the well-being of young people. When the self-description at stake is one that I regard as fundamental to my identity, a willingness to act inconsistently with the self-description indicates that I am not what I thought I was.

Having a character with any content means having some limits, and if I treat every limit as potentially for sale, that is a sign that I lack any real character. Unless some things have been pulled off the table as nonnegotiable, the convictions which I assumed gave my character shape will be mostly illusory. Of course, it may not seem that way to me. But that is because I imagine what I am to be firmly established. With regard to certain features, it is in fact well established, but some elements of my character will be virtually unformed until I have shaped them under pressure. If I have never been tempted to steal, my idea of myself as an honest person may be more of a hope than an indication of anything substantial. When I find myself in a situation where the pressures or incentives are pushing me to go against my principles, I am in a position to determine whether those principles will actually shape who I am.

It is easy to imagine that my identity is resilient enough to maintain itself no matter what I do, but some important features of it are likely to be more fragile than I imagine. To act with integrity means doing what is necessary to keep my reflectively-chosen identity secure. In practice this means treating my identity-conferring affirmations as vitally important, immeasurably more important than any lesser goods I might desire. For the person of integrity the preservation of identity is the precondition which limits and gives direction to all other pursuits.

AN EXAMPLE OF INTEGRITY

Robert Bolt's play, *A Man For All Seasons*, gives a dramatic portrayal of the events leading to the execution of Sir Thomas More in sixteenth-century England. More was Lord Chancellor during the reign of King Henry VIII. He was a distinguished scholar and lawyer, personally acquainted with and well respected by the greatest thinkers in Europe. Conflict with Henry arose over Henry's plan to divorce his wife, Catherine, in order to marry Anne Boleyn. While Henry probably had a variety of reasons, prominent among them was his desire for a male heir. When the Pope refused to annul Henry's marriage, the King finally had Parliament proclaim him head of the Church of England and give official recognition to heirs produced by his union with Anne Boleyn.

More was not eager to face the King's wrath and potential martyrdom. While he rejected the legitimacy of Henry's marriage to Anne, he refrained from making any public or private pronouncements which could be judged treasonable. When the bishops submitted to Henry's claim to be Supreme Head of the Church of England, More quietly resigned his post. However, More's reputation and influence were such that the King regarded his affirmation as vital. Henry attempted to secure this by the Act of Succession which required subjects to swear under oath that the King's marriage to Catherine was invalid. When More refused to take the oath, he was put in prison and stripped of his possessions until he should agree to take it. Deprived of contact with his family who were forced into relative poverty, More continued to resist powerful pressures and incentives to get him to change his mind. Virtually all the prominent men of the kingdom signed the oath, but More steadfastly refused to assent to what he believed false.

To many people More's refusal to go along with the King at

great personal cost to himself and his family is hardly comprehensible. In our day, the swearing of an oath to God in court does not appear to add much credibility to testimony. People routinely expect that when a person has a strong personal stake in some matter, swearing an oath makes it no more likely that the truth will be told.[7] To refuse to swear falsely at the cost of prison and execution is an option that few people today (or in More's time) would be willing to entertain.

It may clarify the issue somewhat to note that More believed that an oath was not a mere formality, but a solemn invocation to God to witness one's words and punish with eternal damnation the person who would swear falsely. A person who genuinely believed this is unlikely to view an oath in court or solemn vows in a marriage ceremony in a light-hearted manner. But in Bolt's portrayal of More, what is at issue is not merely what God may do in the afterlife, but what a person who takes an oath lightly might do to himself.

In the play, More's daughter attempts to persuade him to take the oath and come home to his family. In explaining to her why he cannot More replies, "When a man takes an oath, Meg, he's holding his own self in his hands. Like water.... And if he opens his fingers then—he needn't hope to find himself again."[8] The idea here is that an oath is more than an ordinary promise. To take an oath is to offer yourself as security. If you are willing to pledge your self falsely, then the self that you have to offer amounts to very little. Taking the oath seriously expresses the degree of respect that you have for yourself.

Bolt says that More had

> an adamantine sense of his own self. He knew where he began and left off, what area he could yield to the encroachments of his enemies and what to the encroachments of those he loved...but at length he was asked to retreat from the final area where he located his self...and could no more be budged than a cliff.[9]

After it became evident that More would not change his mind, he was brought to trial and sentenced to death on the strength of perjured testimony. At the trial it was made clear to him that he had only to go along with the pledge virtually all of his noteworthy contemporaries had taken in order to be released and even rewarded. But More dug in his heels and went to his death rather than sacrifice his integrity.

Many people would view this sort of rigid stubbornness as foolish. They would claim that swearing falsely to save yourself and your family is much more reasonable and admirably flexible. But the question More faced was whether there existed some features of the self that he had so identified with that to give them up was to have nothing left worth keeping. The things that a person cannot bring himself to do or could not live with himself if he did are indications of what that person cares about, and some concerns may go so deeply into the self that to lose them would be to lose the evaluative perspective by which the self cares about anything at all.

For More his allegiance to God was an absolutely nonnegotiable component of who he was and what he stood for. It was something he must hold onto at all costs. In the play More challenges the Duke of Norfolk's willingness to go along with the King's demands with the question, "Is there no single sinew in the midst of this that serves no appetite of Norfolk's but is just Norfolk?"[10] Having a self means identifying with something which one has chosen to give priority over any particular appetites. Thus, More affirms that his opposition to the King arises from something inseparable from his identity. He says, "I will not give in because I oppose it—I do—not my pride, not my spleen, nor any of my appetites but *I* do—*I*!"[11] For More the self which shapes and rules the appetites will in the end be all he will have to offer to God. If he lets that self slip through his fingers, he will be empty-handed when he meets his Maker.

TWO FORMS OF INTEGRITY

We can distinguish between two general kinds of cases where it is appropriate to say that an individual acts with integrity. The first type involves a judgment that one's evaluative perspective demands a certain type of action, but this judgment conflicts with strong inclinations to do something else. Though one could yield to these inclinations, instead she sides with the evaluative point of view and overrules the contrary impulses, possibly after an extended struggle.

The second type of case involves a person whose identity has been so strongly integrated that there are no forces powerful enough to put up much of a struggle. Though this person may recognize the advantages of violating a fundamental commitment, she finds herself unable to seriously consider doing so. Because she has identified herself fully with the commitment, violating it is unthinkable for her. She is subject to what Harry Frankfurt calls volitional necessity.

The line between these two kinds of cases is not sharp. One might have a partially-solidified identity which puts a choice somewhere in between the struggle case and the volitional necessity case. Also one might be more or less immune to some kinds of inducements, but susceptible to others. Nevertheless, we can often recognize particular instances of integrity as closer to one category than the other. For example, Thomas More's exercise of integrity appears more like the second type than the first. Whatever the incentives, he simply cannot bring himself to take a false oath.

While there is something admirable about the kind of person who can struggle against recalcitrant impulses and win, a life with too much struggle of this sort indicates serious problems. What if I have to struggle with whether to shoplift virtually every time I go to the store? Or what if I have to struggle about whether to be faithful to my spouse any time I meet an attractive and potentially available sexual partner? It is not only time-consuming, but draining if too many aspects of my identity are up for grabs. The kind of life most of us would aspire to would probably be one where at least some aspects of identity are firmly established without the need to continually reopen closed issues. In other words, we would want many of our actions to be governed by something close to volitional necessity.

In reflectively preferring to be governed by volitional necessity, we are choosing to act in accordance with what we judge to be our deepest concerns. Harry Frankfurt notes that the binding quality of such a restriction on one's volition need not be perceived as constraining:

> The reason a person does not experience the force of volitional necessity as alien or external to himself, is that it coincides with—and is, indeed, partly constituted by—desires which are not merely his own but with which he actively identifies himself. Moreover, the necessity is to a certain extent self-imposed. It is generated when someone requires himself to avoid being guided in what he does by any forces other than those he most deeply wants to be guided by.[12]

To become the kind of person who has built a self with some elements subject to volitional necessity is to take a certain kind of risk. In some circumstances, acting in accordance with basic convictions can mean suffering or death, as it did for More. Or it might mean public scorn and financial ruin as it did for many who opposed officially-sanctioned racism in U.S. society of the 1960s. One who has formed a character which is firm and unbending in some areas may find herself unable to avoid paying the price. If she had known in advance what it might lead to, she would have strongly considered forming a more compliant self. Or would she? For the kind of person we are considering is one who buys into the values which have formed her character and the volitional necessity that goes with affirming those values. In identifying with the evaluation she accepts, she might very well affirm that the risks, however great, were worth taking.

Obviously, not everyone would agree that becoming a person with strong convictions that might lead to suffering is a risk worth taking. But when we try to fill out what kind of life goes with the absence of strong convictions, it is difficult to paint an attractive picture. What, we might wonder, does the person who lacks any firm convictions have to live for? If the answer turns out to be pleasure and the avoidance of pain, we are imagining a life too shallow, too lacking in meaning, and too deprived of the satisfactions that many of us regard vitally important to merit serious consideration. When we reflect on the kind of life we could be pleased with, many of us will find that our conception of a desirable life calls for taking the kind of risk involved in becoming a person of integrity.

INTEGRITY AND SELF-INTEREST

More's thinking when he refuses to take a false oath or Sakharov's thinking when he publicly opposes the authority structure of his society differs from what we usually call self-interested thinking. Given their values and commitments, there is no need to weigh particular gains and losses of potential ways of acting, for the evaluative orientation they have identified with requires some choices and rules out others. In affirming this evaluative orientation each is acting to maintain the self he has, but in each case the concerns that give this self unity are directed toward objects outside the self. In More's case the self gets its coherence through an absolute devotion to God. For Sakharov it is a dedication to human rights that gives his self an abiding center.

There is reason to say that More and Sakharov repeatedly act against their self-interest, and it would clearly sound bizarre to claim that More's acceptance of death was a self-interested choice. We could possibly construe each as acting for the sake of a certain kind of benefit, but it is misleading to put the benefit in question in the same class with other kinds of personal benefits. One who seeks to maintain an identity or self-respect will often be subordinating the kinds of considerations that we usually identify with the individual's interest in order to give priority to concerns for things that are external to the self. If people such as More or Sakharov are pursuing their own interest, it is their interest in being the kind of self that is not predominantly concerned with its own interest.

To be motivated by integrity is either to move beyond self-interest or to redefine what constitutes self-interest in a way that turns it into something very different. When one's interest is connected with acting in accordance with certain principles that may not be personally advantageous or acting to produce some benefit to others, even when it involves personal sacrifice, it has been transformed in such a way that the contrast between self-interested behavior and behavior from other motivations is no longer clear. But perhaps this is just what we should expect in a well- integrated self.

For most of us the line between self-interest and other sorts of motivations is sharp because we have divided allegiances. We can distinguish between doing something to bring ourselves recognition and doing it because we think we ought to. But this is because in our experience these motivations sometimes push us in different directions, and our priorities are not clearly defined. We care about doing what we ought, but we also care about getting personal benefits for ourselves, and sometimes we find ourselves opting for one concern at the expense of the other. For a person who has integrated moral concerns into the self, the conflict is different. Obligations and virtues are essential features of the self, not optional components. They are not in competition with concerns for personal benefits. Rather the concerns for personal benefits are concerns of a self that is formed by particular obligations and character traits. Such a self may still have temptations, but these temptations can be recognized as threats to unified identity.

We can imagine someone like More saying that it is in his interest to do what will result in prison or execution. But these are interests of a self that has a clearly defined moral identity. One who is able to think of his interest in this way has gone a long way towards resolving the conflicts that indicate a divided self, but not everyone is willing to pay such a price to obtain this kind of resolution.

SELF-DECEPTION

A more common way to deal with dividedness is through self-deception. All of us form some conception of our identity, and when we become aware of something which threatens this conception, we can be strongly tempted to hide it from ourselves. By concealing painful truths from ourselves, we maintain the illusion of identity and avoid having to confront the reality of fragmentation.

While self-deception is widely acknowledged as a fact of human psychology, it sometimes seems puzzling that there could be such a thing. It is easy enough to understand how one person might deceive another person. But how could the same individual be both deceiver and deceived? To be deceiver one needs to know the truth, but if you know the truth, how can you hide it from yourself and become a victim of deception?

Herbert Fingarette suggests the following account: There are skilled performances by means of which an individual is able to spell out things in consciousness or become explicitly aware of them. However, much that we are aware of is not explicitly spelled out, and in some cases we have a motivation for not spelling out what we are aware of. One kind of motivation arises from a conflict between our conception of ourselves and engagements which do not fit with the self we have posited. So self-deception in these cases is a way of retaining conflicting elements which do not fit together without having to face up to an acknowledgment that might be painful.

A woman had her marriage broken when her husband had an affair with another woman. She became understandably angry with both her husband and with the woman she accused of "stealing" her husband. A few months after the divorce she was gratified when an attractive male coworker began showing her a great deal of attention. Responding to the interest of this coworker, whom she knew to be married, she began a sexual involvement. During the time of her affair, she never thought of what she was doing as adultery, and though she had spent long months railing against "the other woman," it never occurred to her that she had chosen to become the other woman.

Our capacities for ignoring the obvious are great, and when an acknowledgment might prove devastating it is understandable why we might engage in some self-protection. But the refusal to be honest with ourselves comes at the cost of increased fragmentation of our identity. Trying to hold together a self-image that offers comfort, but conflicts with what we are at some level aware of, can try our ingenuity and raise our anxiety level. Furthermore, when we rely on self-deception as a strategy, we tend to need more and more of it to maintain our comfort level. Putting bandaids on an identity that is showing signs of fracture may keep things going for a while, but it tends to prolong and magnify the underlying problem.

A divorced father who shows little interest in his children's lives and makes no effort to spend time with them, but sends the court-ordered child support, tells himself that he is a good parent. A manager, whom employees tiptoe around because of her volatile temper and whom everyone says is a bear to work for, prides herself on her skill in human relations. A student who makes only perfunctory efforts to study blames his poor grades on quirky professors who make unfair tests. Many of us are skilled at figuring out ways to refuse to take responsibility for our actions. We feel misunderstood by those who are less willing to interpret what we do so charitably, and we selectively construe the evidence to put the best face on what we have done.

Of course, some degree of giving ourselves the benefit of the doubt is probably called for, and often actions are capable of multiple interpretation. But our self-deceptive strategies go beyond the bounds of arguable opinion, for we view ourselves in ways that the facts we are aware of do not permit. Unfortunately, the more we rely on these strategies, the less we are able to attain the kind of realistic self-assessment that would allow us to make the adjustments needed to achieve the life we want. As long as we fail to acknowledge the ways our actions conflict with our self-image, we will avoid taking the steps necessary to assert control over our lives.

An ideal that most of us would affirm is a harmony between the activities of a person and the person's self-understanding. That ideal is more of a goal to pursue than an achievement we can expect to accomplish completely. Even the best integrated person is likely to have some pockets of self-deception. However, by nurturing the kind of self-awareness that removes the foothold of self-deception, we can hope to move closer to the goal.

One way to enhance self-awareness is to live in the kind of

community where others will tell you what you need to hear. There are things about you that friends and acquaintances know well, but are unlikely to reveal to someone who is unreceptive. Cultivating an attitude of openness toward your friends' observations and seeking the kinds of friends who are willing to hold you accountable for your actions (and omissions) are vital means for gaining insight about yourself. Often what people call friendship or love is a weak imitation of the kind of relationship in which we are mutually committed to encouraging the development of our better selves.

Along with the discipline of community go individual habits of reflection in which we learn to see our lives from a broader and less biased perspective. It is easy to develop self-serving interpretations of events and fail to take into account facts that might contribute to a more balanced understanding. When you got so angry at the auto service manager over the delay at repairing your car, you may have felt some gratification at letting loose your righteous indignation. But what was the issue like from his perspective? Was the dispute really as clear-cut as it seemed? By pulling back to think of our concerns in relation to the concerns of others, we can often see more clearly what is at stake. Cultivating the habit of doing this is a fundamental tool for combating self-deception. (For some religious people the activity that helps one pull back to a less biased assessment is prayer. A serious effort to pray involves attempting to see things from God's point of view.)

No tool is foolproof. But through the right sort of community and sustained habits of personal reflection we can attempt to remind ourselves of what it is we want to be and measure our actions according to how well they fit with our aspirations. Our best efforts may fall short, but without diligent attention and effort, our identity may fall apart.

Chapter Eleven

SELF-TRANSFORMATION

Living according to an ideal is a project in self-transformation. For when we are guided by an ideal, we not only satisfy wants, but also strengthen or weaken our dispositions, and thereby shape our characters. We are endeavoring to become the kinds of persons our ideals represent. (John Kekes[1])

Self-creation is a matter of shaping our characteristics, even minor ones in the light of our attitudes and values. (Jonathan Glover[2])

... the quality of our lives is a function not only of what we get but also of what we are. And what we are, no less than what we get, depends on what we choose. (David Schmidtz[3])

One kind of control over your life is the freedom to do what you want. However, what if you realize that what you want to do is not good for you, that it will probably make you miserable, yet you still want it? Would acting according to *that* want indicate that you are in control of your life? In such a case, following your wants seems more like being under their power. To genuinely take charge of your life, you need a deeper kind of control: control over your wants.

Gaining control over your wants is only possible when you can distinguish yourself from your desires. Suppose that you have a strong, perhaps even an overpowering desire to smoke, but as you think about the place of smoking in your life, you judge that it would be better if you did not have such a desire, or at least that it was not so strong. Your judgment reflects an evaluative perspective that is distinct from your desire. In this case, establishing a deeper control over your life would mean being able to overrule your desire and act in accordance with your evaluative judgment. The ability to do so allows you to put your desires in service of the kind of life you seek to have.

However, it would be difficult to achieve your conception of a desirable life if your desires are constantly at war with your evaluative judgments. If you expect to act consistently with your judgments, you will need to bring your desires into some degree of harmony with them. If you cannot immediately erase your desire to smoke, you may be able to weaken it and develop a strategy to replace it eventually with other desires that you can reflectively endorse. By such a process you would be moving closer to what I called in previous chapters a unified identity.

Creating such an identity is a project in self-transformation. A person who attempts to modify his desires, dispositions, habits, attitudes, and so forth. is shaping the self to bring about a greater harmony between its characteristics and the evaluative perspective he identifies with. While the ideal of perfect harmony is probably an impossible dream, altering the self to bring about greater unity is an essential part of attempting to live in accordance with a reflectively chosen conception of a desirable life.

Most of what we do is initiated by a motivational structure that functions independently of our capacity to stand back and reflect on how a particular action will contribute to the kind of life we are seeking. Most of the time we will be motivated by friendship or ambition or the desire for recognition or anger or some other particular impulse. A project of self-transformation cannot and should not try to replace the more or less spontaneous sources of action. To do so would leave us paralyzed and ineffective. What is needed is to develop and encourage certain impulses and to modify or extinguish others so that the motivational structure can, by and large, produce actions that the reflective self can approve of.

In considering the direction of my life, I might discern a need to increase my capacity to act out of loving concern for those close to me or to decrease my tendency to sulk when things don't go my way. What I should aim at is not making all my behavior cool and calculating, but rather cultivating the motivational springs that will contribute to the sort of life I am seeking. As I try to develop a friendly attitude or an interest in literature or a passion for justice, I am unleashing something that will take on a life of its own. The job of the reflective self is not to replace that life, but to try to encourage the kinds of impulses that will lead to a satisfying fulfillment of reflectively discerned inclinations, talents, values, and dreams.

Some writers have used the term "self-creation" to refer to our ability to form the self. This metaphor can suggest an exaggerated picture of our powers. We should not imagine that we can exempt ourselves from the forces of heredity and environment, and the self of the evaluative perspective will be subject to a variety of limitations we do not choose. Furthermore, we cannot produce every alteration that might seem desirable. However, thinking in terms of molding or shaping ourselves can be helpful in reminding us of a power which is vitally important and easily neglected.

By the company we keep, the jobs we do, and the leisure activities we pursue, we shape ourselves. When our choices are informed by our picture of the kind of person we are striving to be, we take charge of our lives. We may not always know how each type of engagement will affect us, but sometimes it is clear that a certain friendship or group involvement or commitment is likely to bring our activities into greater alignment with our ideals and alter our concerns in a desirable direction. By cultivating an awareness of where the various processes we submit ourselves to are leading, we increase our potential control over the formation of the self.

Admittedly, much of what we become is not consciously shaped. We do not and probably cannot effectively evaluate how each of our actions will affect us. However, it is possible to exercise a much greater control over what we become than we commonly do, and the alternative to asserting control is to allow ourselves to be shaped more or less haphazardly. While we cannot mold ourselves into anything that we might choose, we can through conscious choice move ourselves in directions that are conducive to building the sort of life we aspire to have.

THE POWER OF PRETENDING

There is a fairy tale in which an evil man seeks to win the heart of a beautiful princess in order to marry her. He enlists the help of a sorcerer who makes for him a magic mask. This mask will hide all the signs of evil in his face, and the unsuspecting princess will see the appearance of an honorable and caring man that she could love. However, the sorcerer warns the man that once he puts on the mask, he must pretend to have the qualities that the mask shows. If he fails to act in a loving and kind manner, the mask will shatter and reveal the evil person that he is.

So agreeing to these conditions, the evil man puts on the magic mask, and his features are transformed. With the help of this device he meets and courts the beautiful princess and wins her love. Always careful to act in ways that will maintain his disguise, the evil man marries the princess and acts the part of a good and loving husband. The two have a blissful fairy-tale marriage, but after many years the evil man becomes troubled by his deception. He realizes that the love he has won under false pretenses is not really love for him at all, but only for the man he has been pretending to be. He longs for the love of his wife, but he cannot have it by wearing the mask. After months of inner conflict, he finally decides to remove the mask and show the princess his true self. She may leave him, but anything would be better than the agony he now endures. So he takes off the mask, and underneath it is revealed a face that is indistinguishable from the person he has been pretending to be.

The story portrays a remarkable psychological truth. Actions shape character. What we do over time creates inner habits and traits which correspond to our behavior. If we act consistently as a courageous person would, we become courageous. If we repeatedly act in caring fashion toward other people, we become caring individuals. Similarly, if we do harmful acts, we become cruel and malicious What we become is a product of the way we act over time.

But in the story the evil man was only pretending to be good. Nevertheless, if the pretense could be total enough, it would shape him. The part he is playing is not one where he sneaks off to do evil deeds in his spare time. He is instead spending all his efforts to conform perfectly to the role. In the end he becomes like the person he is pretending to be because the traits he needs to sustain his performance are indistinguishable from those of a genuinely good person.

Of course, it's a fairy tale. It takes magic for an evil person to play a role that conflicts so greatly with the traits he has actually developed. But while we should not expect this dramatic a transformation in real life, we can still recognize that actions have a powerful influence on character. To develop the character traits we want, we need to act as we would if we already had them.

Some may find this suggestion problematic. If I am not now compassionate or generous, how can I do the compassionate or generous actions that will produce these traits in me? I may occasionally be able to do some things which imitate what a person with these traits might do. But imitating compassion is not the same as acting out of compassion. For example, part of being compassionate is feeling something for the person in need, and if I act to help someone, but don't feel the appropriate emotions, my actions are not genuinely compassionate. I will be going through the motions, and a really discerning person might be able to tell that I was faking it. Telling me to act in accordance with traits I don't have is like telling me to learn the skills of heart surgery by going out and operating on a few hearts. I need the skills before I do the surgery.

The basic distinction underlying this objection is correct. There is a difference between acting out of a complex character trait and doing something which resembles what the possessor of the trait might do. You might do what a generous person would do without doing it out of generosity. A character trait of this sort will involve intellectual and emotional characteristics that produce the observable behavior, and the kind of discernment needed to see what should be done on a given occasion depends in part on some of the hidden characteristics that shape the awareness of the possessor of the trait. It is unlikely that a mere imitator will be able to duplicate entirely what a person with a well developed character could do.

However, to take the heart-surgery analogy seriously, the essential question is not whether a novice could duplicate the actions of a skilled performer; it is whether a beginner might develop the skills needed to engage in the performance herself. We can imagine a doctor being asked to perform heart surgery before she had adequate knowledge and skills, but the preparation to do your own surgery must at least include some practice at doing surgery. Perhaps one practices constituent elements of the operation before trying to put them all together, and we might hope that an initial attempt would be under the instruction and guidance of a skilled practitioner, but ultimately there is no substitute for doing it yourself. You develop the skill by practice.

It is the same with any skilled performance. You don't expect to be able to play a Beethoven sonata when you have just started to take lessons. But given some raw ability and decent instruction, you may get to the point where you are ready for something more advanced that will test your skills. You have to start out playing the scales and doing the finger exercises that will help you internalize desirable habits. If you stick with it, much that you initially had to concentrate on directly will be done without thinking while you focus on something else. But it is essentially by doing that you develop the relevant skills.

So when it is suggested that you learn to be compassionate by doing what a compassionate person would do, we could take this to be similar to the suggestion that you learn how to play tennis by imitating the strokes your instructor shows you. You do not start with the kind of physical and mental habits underlying the instructor's performance, but by repeated attempts to imitate the example and to correct your mistakes, you may gradually come to internalize similar habits which enable you to consistently do what you need in competition.

Even so, it might be objected, part of the problem with character traits is that they involve emotions and habits of thought, and while we might learn to act in ways that resemble the compassionate person, that does not mean we think and feel as this person does. This objection is more impressive if we are thinking of an immediate change rather than a gradual process. Moreover, it underestimates the connection between actions and patterns of thought and feeling. There is considerable evidence to show that our actions strongly affect the way we think and consequently the way we feel. As one psychologist puts it,

> If social psychologists have proven anything during the last thirty years, they have proven that the actions we elect leave a residue inside us. Every time we act, we amplify the underlying idea or tendency. Most people presume ... that our traits and attitudes affect our behavior. That is true ... But it's also true that our traits and attitudes *follow* our behavior. We are as likely to *act ourselves into a new way of thinking* as to think ourselves into a new way of acting.[4]

Salespeople know that if they can get you to answer questions related to a product they are selling, they are much more likely to get an attentive consideration. It is as if you interpret your own participation as a kind of tacit interest and adjust your behavior to the kind of interest you think you have exhibited. People tend to think in ways that provide reasons for the ways they act. So if you are acting consistently in accordance with some character trait, you are likely to adjust your thinking in a way that fits the trait.

To a large extent your feelings will reflect your thoughts and concerns. If you are behaving in compassionate ways and learning to pay attention to things that a compassionate person would notice, the long-term result should be the development of compassionate feelings. These sorts of feelings generally arise in a person who becomes vividly aware of the suffering of others. When you are actively involved in helping people, it is necessary to pay attention to their situation and become aware of what they need. This way of thinking is necessary for doing a good imitation of compassionate action, yet it is precisely the kind of thinking which will tend to evoke an emotional response in a normal person. Some people are more naturally empathetic and aware of what it is like for others, but even people who have only minimal tendencies in this direction can usually increase the level of awareness that will evoke an emotional response by adjusting what they attend to.

So the power of pretending is that when we alter our patterns of behavior to imitate the kind of living we aspire to, we bring about changes in the self conducive to this way of living. This principle applies not just to character traits, but to personality traits as well. There are probably strong genetic predispositions to having an introverted or an extraverted personality. But these predispositions do not prevent a person from intentionally altering patterns of behavior that she finds herself prone to. If I decide that I need to be a bit more outgoing, my initial step may be to try out some outgoing behaviors: making eye contact, introducing myself to strangers, expressing interest in what others are talking about. These attempts may initially be awkward, but with practice I am likely to become more comfortable with them. I may still prefer to stay home and read a book alone, but I need not think of myself as a permanent victim of my genetic or socially-acquired tendencies.

If this sort of change is difficult, it is in part because it is difficult to alter established habits. We regulate our lives by countless habits which we are scarcely aware of. Most people have regular ways of getting dressed, but could not tell you which sock or pants leg they put on first without watching themselves. In the case of a skill such as bicycle riding (or even walking) there are internalized muscular habits that are beyond our awareness. To alter an established habit, we have to consciously behave in a contrary way over an extended period of time until a new habit is established.

Suppose that I realize that my relationships have been hampered by my bad listening habits. When others are speaking, I am not really paying attention, but instead thinking about what I want to say and how I can direct the conversation to my interests. As a result, my acquaintances don't feel comfortable with the kind of disclosure that a close relationship requires. When my failings are called to my attention, I think about how I can change this habitual pattern of interaction. I practice giving full attention to what someone has said to the point of being able to summarize it in a way that shows I have understood that person's concern. I suppress any urges to interrupt or to change the subject until I am sure the topic raised by the other person has been adequately explored. When someone tells about an experience she had, I don't immediately jump in and tell about a similar experience of mine, but show interest in her experience. To change my conversational style, it is not enough just to know about an alternative. If I don't put my new principles into practice, I won't develop my ability to use the new style. Furthermore, it is only by internalizing my new set of habits through practice that I will be able to avoid reverting to established ones.

Of course, the more firmly established we are in our habits, the more difficult change becomes. William James writes, "Could the young but realize how soon they will become walking bundles of habits, they would give more heed to their conduct while in the plastic state. We are spinning our own fates for good or evil..."[5] If we can accumulate a fund of desirable habits, we are freed from nonproductive struggles and enabled to devote our attention to more important matters. By not making everything a matter of choice, we enlarge our range of options over things that matter most.

BAD HABITS

The general principle that actions shape what we become applies not just to desirable traits, but to undesirable ones as well. If I give in to my fears this time, it will be harder to control them next time. If I learn to respond to difficult tasks with procrastination, I may eventually find that I am locked into a pattern that keeps me from getting vital work done. If I repeatedly refuse to attend to the needs of others, I can develop a kind of hardened sensitivity that blocks my capacities for relationship.

Just as we learn virtues by acting in accordance with them, we learn vices by doing the sort of thing a person with the vice would do. The way to become a dishonest person is to do dishonest deeds. The way to become greedy is to act out of greed. The way to become lazy is to practice laziness. In each case the behavior will tend to reinforce the patterns that it exhibits, and repeated action in accordance with the pattern solidifies the trait.

In the same way that desirable behavior alters our thoughts and feelings, undesirable behavior does so as well. In the famous Milgram experiments ordinary people were induced by experimenters to give what they believed were 450-volt electric shocks to a screaming victim. The experiment used a series of steps to get subjects to this point. At first the subjects were told to give a minor shock (15 volts) to a "learner" who failed to answer a question correctly. The severity was increased in small increments. When the learner first showed signs of pain, experimental subjects had already given five shocks and become accustomed to following instructions of an insistent experimenter. Following the tendency to seek reasons for what we are doing, the subjects often came to think of the victim as obstinate and deserving of the shock. Fully 65 percent of participants in the experiment were induced to go all the way to 450 volts.

When you engage in behavior that is at odds with your self-image, it often proceeds in small steps. You start out with a slight hesitation, but everyone assures you that it's nothing to worry about, and the deviation seems relatively minor. From that minor deviation, it may not be a long jump to something slightly more serious, but you think that if you could justify the first step, you can justify this one. At some point along the way, you may dimly perceive that you are getting in over your head, and it may seem necessary to take new steps to cover up deeds you are uneasy about. By such small steps people can find themselves doing things that they would never have imagined they would do. In cases of spectacular scandals which make headline news, it is not uncommon for parties who are caught to be astonished at their own behavior, thinking, "How could I have done such a thing?"

Part of the answer to this question is that the small steps got them gradually accustomed to behaviors for which they could find arguable justifications. But in taking these small steps they were loosening some old habits and establishing some new ones. If conscience reared its ugly head, it was not so difficult to push it down and direct their attention elsewhere. So by a process in which each new step seemed to commit one to go further, a person who thought of himself as a decent, law-abiding citizen found himself involved in tax fraud or insider trading or taking illegal kickbacks, or even murder.

There is a natural human tendency to be shortsighted, to see clearly the immediate pressures and incentives, but only obscurely the long-term consequences of behavior. This tendency is nowhere more evident than in our disregard of the importance of habits we are establishing. We think that a minor lapse to a reflectively chosen policy is insignificant, concentrating on the observable effects of the individual act, but ignoring the possible effects on us. But one of the effects of allowing minor lapses is to establish a habit of allowing lapses. Suppose an executive has adopted a strict policy of refusing any gifts which might create a conflict of interest. But then she is offered a gift that she wants badly to accept. She realizes that this violates her policy, but talks herself into it on the grounds that she will be careful not to let it affect her decisions with regard to the gift-giver. Her willingness to violate her policy increases the likelihood that she will set the policy aside in future cases. She can always think, "It wasn't so bad last time, so I can do it this time too." The potential for erosion of a valuable policy should be evident.

The thinking involved in such a case resembles that of the addict who thinks he can quit any time he wants. William James comments on a play in which a drunken Rip Van Winkle excuses each new round of drinking with the thought, "I won't count this time." Says James,

> Well! he may not count it, and a kind Heaven may not count it; but it is being counted none the less. Down among his nerve cells and fibres the molecules are counting it, registering and storing it up to be used against him when the next temptation comes.[6]

Our actions will transform us whether we recognize it or not. If we can liberate ourselves by developing desirable habits, we can also bind ourselves by developing undesirable ones. Though it is seldom apparent in an individual case, even minor deviations can count for more than we realize.

THE POWER OF ADMIRATION

Nathaniel Hawthorne's short story, "The Great Stone Face," tells of a valley in which people live within view of a huge natural rock formation on the side of a mountain that resembles a human face. As a young boy, Ernest looks with fascination at this face and hears the local legends that some day a man who resembles the Great Stone Face will come to the valley. As the years pass, people become excited from time to time when some native of the valley who had gone away and made a name for himself is about to return, thinking that the native son will soon fulfill the ancient prophecy.

Expectation is high when a very wealthy and successful businessman returns, but when Ernest sees the man, it is obvious to him that there is no resemblance to the magnificent visage of the Great Stone Face. A famous General comes to the valley, and again Ernest is disappointed. Years later a successful politician visits, but despite universal acclaim, the politician is not the long-awaited fulfillment.

During this time Ernest has never lost his fascination with the Great Stone Face. After his daily work was done, he would gaze for hours at the face in which he saw an unmatched nobility, kindness and wisdom. Over the years, as Ernest meditated on and received inspiration from this image, he grew into a man of deep feeling and great wisdom. In offering his wisdom to others he became well-known, attracting visitors from far away who came to seek his council. One day Ernest is visited by a poet whose work he has admired. As Ernest is speaking to the people in an outdoor setting, the poet, looking at the mountain in a moment of inspiration shouts, "Ernest is himself the likeness of the Great Stone Face."[7]

Hawthorne's story suggests that we become like what we deeply love and admire. The hours in which Ernest focused his attention and adoration on the Great Stone Face bore fruit in his life as he took on the qualities he saw in the face. As his attention was engaged by an embodiment of admirable ideals, he absorbed the ideals into his being and without realizing it, came to resemble the object of his love.

I have spoken in earlier chapters of aspiring to live a certain type of life. What I mean by aspiration involves some conception of a desirable life to which an individual responds with admiration and attraction. When we see in a particular way of living something of value and beauty that attracts us, we may either nurture that attraction or neglect it. To the extent that we attend to it and allow our admiration to develop, we have a potentially powerful motivation to shape ourselves in accordance with the values we have come to care about.

In the case of Ernest, the transformative power of his object of admiration apparently worked without his conscious effort. Although he did not know that he was taking on the qualities which had absorbed his attention, his admiration still shaped his concerns in a way that pulled him in the direction of his ideal. However, we can also imagine a process that in addition involves a conscious attempt to emulate a pattern of life that a person admires and is drawn toward. By striving to imitate the pattern that attracts us, we increase the likelihood of producing that pattern in our lives.

In most cases the ideals that constitute an admirable way of life are taken from a person's communal traditions. In some cases these ideals are exemplified in specific individuals. We can imagine Mother Teresa reflecting on the example of Jesus as she adopted her ideal of service to the poor of Calcutta. A Buddhist might find a model of spiritual wisdom and detachment from desire in the life of Gautama Buddha. Plato's inspiration for a philosophic way of life arose from his admiration of Socrates. Whatever the particular model, when ideals become objects of admiration which capture our attention, they can provide a powerful impetus to transform ourselves in accordance with the pattern we admire.

We are shaped by what we love. Our loves may produce a unified life that we can reflectively admire. However, we can also have loves that fragment us, pulling us toward patterns of living that we find unsatisfying. We may love the fulfillment of desires that are inconsistent with our own conception of our better selves. A project of self-transformation involves learning to harmonize our loves with ideals for the self that we love more deeply. By this process we may hope to approximate an order in our lives that more closely matches our aspirations.

SELF-TRANSFORMATION AND HAPPINESS

A project of self-transformation is hard work. Trying to mold yourself in accordance with your ideals and to keep guard over the traits you acquire demands considerable attentiveness, reflectiveness, and persistence. It is easy to see how a person might become distracted from such an enterprise or discouraged by its repeated demands. Given the difficulties, we can well understand why some people might want to opt out of such a project, saying in effect, "I don't really care about what kind of self I become. I just want to get a moderate amount of happiness from life."

So should we view the pursuit of happiness as an alternative to the task of self-transformation? Before drawing such a conclusion, we would do well to reflect on an ancient piece of wisdom: Happiness is not the sort of goal we can pursue directly. We seek happiness by becoming concerned about things other than happiness. As a person fills her life with meaningful work and fulfilling relationships and opportunities for creativity and appreciation of the joys of everyday living, she may on reflection realize that she is happy. But happiness arises through involvement in activities in which an individual finds something of worth. It is more of a by-product of engaging in such activities than an object which can be pursued in isolation.

So to seek happiness one needs to care about a variety of things that can focus her energy toward satisfying activities. By coming to care about our friends and our work, we discover doors to happiness. By becoming interested in philosophy or backpacking, we make possible satisfying engagements which can contribute to happiness. By becoming aware of and attending to the beauty of a sunset or the inquiring mind of a child or a moment of tenderness, we invite happiness into our lives. But all of these pathways to happiness depend upon being the kind of self who cares about and is engaged by the objects that can evoke our capacity for happiness. Hence, the person who says, "I only want a little happiness," needs to give enough attention to the self to preserve and enhance the kinds of concerns and interests that can be expected to produce a happy life.

Furthermore, for most people a happy life would require more than just a collection of activities that are individually satisfying. For example, I might judge my life unhappy if it lacked significant relationships with other people, despite the presence of other goods. Or I might find that though I have things that give me satisfaction, my failure to develop my mind has left me with a fairly narrow range of interests which leave me unfulfilled. Or I might be dissatisfied with my life because I have not achieved anything that I regard as worthwhile or because I have frittered away my talents. In other words a person's satisfaction with life as a whole might depend upon whether or not it measured up to some criteria of a good life. So when one claims to be interested in happiness, but uninterested in what the self becomes, we can ask whether a particular kind of self is needed for living the sort of life that individual could find satisfying.

A person with some depth and reflectiveness is unlikely to be satisfied with a life in which actions fail to embody her most considered valuations. If I am acutely aware that my pattern of living is at odds with my own conception of a worthwhile kind of life, it is hard to be pleased with my life or to regard myself as happy. I may avoid awareness by exercising self-deception or by failing to develop a coherent evaluative perspective. But the solutions of self-deception or shallowness are hardly appealing.

Perhaps, though, there is another way of understanding the person who wants to opt out of self-transformation. Such an individual might be saying that her reflective judgments of what is valuable do not contain any ideals of human development or of individual development. Instead she conceives a good life as one with more pleasures than pains. So as long as she is able to enjoy the pleasures that life presents and minimize the pains, she will be happy.

My response to this claim is twofold: First, some self-development is required even for this kind of life. It takes some discipline and self-control to effectively pursue pleasures and avoid pains. Second, what we are imagining is a life that most people, on reflective consideration, would find greatly impoverished. The discussions in Part Two of this book on choosing a self show some of the possibilities that anyone content with such a life would be closing off. While I am not arguing that it is necessarily inconsistent to want such a life, I do claim that most people who reflectively consider a wider range of options will aspire to more.

The task of self-transformation is essentially a matter of bringing your aspirations and your actions together. It is trying to become the kind of person who cares about the things that you yourself regard as important. It means shaping the self's motivations to be able to live the kind of life that you think worth living. It is not a guarantee of happiness, but without it the kind of happiness available may turn out to be deeply disappointing. By seeking to become in reality the person you aspire to be, you are attempting to unify an identity that is fragmented and incomplete. If you are successful, you will become a self whose way of living expresses your own deepest concerns.

Conclusion

BEYOND SELF-INTEREST

When we push our self-interested thinking far enough, we bump up against the limits of self-interest. One source of these limits arises from what a total commitment to the pursuit of self-interest would do to us. Suppose I decide that in every action I will try to benefit myself as much as possible. In order to follow my plan consistently, I need to become the kind of person who cares more about getting benefits for myself than anything else. I must avoid coming to care too much about anything that could distract me from the pursuit of my benefit. So I have to make sure that I do not become too attached to other people or too involved in pursuing goals that might not coincide with getting all I can for myself. In short, my plan calls for me to narrow my range of concerns so I can remain focused on my single-minded quest.

It does not take a great deal of insight to realize that I have just developed a recipe for living a fairly unsatisfying life. By developing the kind of detachment needed for eliminating competitors to personal benefit, I have excluded many of the passionate concerns that might have produced deep engagement with life. In trying to focus so exclusively on my self-interest, I have removed much of the substantive content that could have given me something to live for.

So where did I go wrong? Perhaps I went wrong in thinking that the way to promote my interest is by making a concern for my interest the motivation for every act. For in becoming the kind of person who is preeminently concerned with getting as much as possible, I effectively marginalize all those benefits that depend on being concerned about things other than myself. For example, the benefits of love and friendship come from caring about and committing myself to other people. If I try to govern my relationships by self-interested calculations of what I am getting and what I am giving in return, I sow the seeds for destroying those relationships and whatever benefits they might have provided. The style of thought that might be useful for regulating my investments can easily lead to bankruptcy in my personal life.

Similarly, many of the enjoyments that people find deeply satisfying depend on forgetting about enjoyment and becoming absorbed in something else. The person who is likely to get the most out of music is not someone who is obsessed with getting the most. It is someone who can forget about how much she is getting and lose herself in the music. The person who will find the deepest satisfaction in scientific work is not someone whose attention is directed toward personal rewards, but someone who develops a passionate interest in the work. Being too concerned about what we can get effectively blocks us from getting some of the satisfactions and enjoyments that people find most fulfilling.

So even a superficial attempt to think about self-interest ought to lead us to recognize the importance of developing involvements and concerns that are independent of a concern for receiving benefits. If self-interested motivations are allowed to squeeze out every other kind of motive, the result will be a life that is impoverished with regard to many of the benefits that we usually associate with living a quality life. A self that is motivated exclusively by a concern to get as much as she can will be unable to get many of the things that matter most.

Perhaps, then, what I need is a conception of self-interest that permits me to do what is likely to bring about a quality life for myself. Instead of saying that I will try to make every action yield the most benefit for me, I could attempt to build into myself the kinds of interests and concerns that will enable me to become deeply engaged with life. If I regard capacities to appreciate and enjoy certain types of experiences to be crucial to the sort of life I want, I will consider the development and exercise of these capacities to be in my interest. If thinking about what is in my interest in certain contexts hampers my aim of obtaining a quality life, I will learn to substitute those modes of thought which are more congenial to achieving the desired way of life.

If I operate under this less direct approach to self-interest, it is important to recognize that, depending on my conception of a quality life, I may be developing motivations and practices which will sometimes be at odds with my assessments of what would yield the greatest benefit for me. For example, if I develop concerns for other people strong enough to support loving relationships, I may sometimes be motivated to do what is needed for someone I care about, even at the expense of satisfying significant needs and desires for personal gain. In pursuing the goal of a desirable life, I am taking into myself motivations which can operate independently of my concern for my interest and which may conflict with self-interested motivations. So this sort of thinking about self-interest leads to a paradoxical kind of limit on self-interest. If I pursue my interest in living a quality life, I may become the kind of person who will not always be motivated to act in accordance with what I judge to be in my self-interest.

Suppose, for instance, that in seeking to live out my conception of a desirable life, I develop a deep attachment and commitment to another person. Because I love her, I may be able to regard most actions aimed at her benefit as benefits for me as well. But acting for her good will sometimes be at the expense of doing what benefits me most. I might, for example, give up significant career opportunities in order to advance her career. If I really love her, I will sometimes be motivated to seek her benefit even when it does not coincide with mine. Furthermore, in becoming the kind of person who is motivated by a concern for her good, I may sometimes find myself psychologically incapable of seeking my own benefit. For example, I might be unable to abandon my disabled spouse even though I give up a great deal to devote myself to her care.[1]

Clearly, then, there is a significant difference between asking what individual act promotes my self-interest and asking what kind of self-formation can contribute to the kind of life I seek. If I devote myself to making each act promote my interest, I will very likely hamper my chance to get the sort of life that satisfies me. However, if I shift my efforts to try to become the kind of person who might lead a satisfying life, I may discover that the motivational structure I develop is not always conducive to acting for my self-interest. So my self-interested thinking, when pursued far enough, may lead me to develop motivations which take me beyond self-interest.

A DESIRABLE LIFE

The line of thought which pushes self-interest beyond itself depends on some conception of what kind of life is desirable. I have argued throughout this book that a conception of a desirable life is not the product of self-interested thought, but results from a different type of thinking which provides a context necessary for coherently applying our judgments about self-interest. Once I have a conception of a desirable life, I can think about the best way to attain it. But my conception will be built out of considerations such as what I admire, what I judge valuable or important, what I think human fulfillment consists of, and what my inclinations and talents make possible. These considerations cannot be reduced to determinations of self-interest. Instead they furnish the background framework needed for defining what is in my interest and making its pursuit a sensible goal.

Although living out one's conception of a desirable life may sometimes mean acting against self-interest, the conception will also regulate and modify judgments of self-interest to bring them closer to the motivating forces such a life requires. For example, someone whose conception of a quality life included certain ideals of friendship might judge betraying a friend for a large sum of money not to be beneficial. This is not to say that she could not be tempted to violate her ideals; it is to say that going after the money would be acting against her better judgment of what is good for her, for her good is defined in relation to maintaining the kind of self needed for living the life she aspires to live. Benefits which are inconsistent with being able to live this type of life are not benefits for her.

In general, when an act threatens the integrity of the self needed for living someone's conception of a desirable life, it is not in the interest of that person to do it. Hence, maintaining one's integrity might be thought of as self-interested, however, being motivated by integrity is very different from other types of self-interested motivation. What is being sought is not some ordinary benefit, but preservation of the kind of self essential to living a particular type of life. One who is motivated to act with integrity in effect opts out of measuring particular gains or losses, treating the preservation of the self as an all-important precondition to the pursuit of benefits. For the person of integrity standard calculations of benefits become irrelevant when the self is at stake.

In one way or another the self is always at stake. Even if a particular act poses no great threat to the self, it may contribute to a pattern which is forming the desired kind of self or sabotaging that formation. When we view self-interest from the perspective of the kind of life we are seeking, the pursuit of any kind of benefit is regulated by considerations of how that benefit and the way it is pursued fits into the overall way of life. So, for example, a physician who aspires to live by an ideal of service to the patient might realize that the actual conduct of her work is instead dominated by business concerns. Whether because of a system which pressures her in this direction or because of an unrecognized greed, her activities conflict with her ideals. If she wishes to maintain her ideals, she needs to modify her outlook and her actions so as to preserve the kind of self required to support the life she aspires to have.

When our conception of a desirable life involves concerns for things beyond the self, we move beyond self-interest. Some people move only a little beyond self-interest, but there are people who take into the self concerns which direct their attention outward. Even if we imagine these people to be motivated to live as they do because of a concern to achieve happiness or fulfillment, it is important to notice that some people's conception of happiness involves forming a self that has its attention absorbed by things remote from its own benefit. Suppose that Mother Teresa reflectively decides that she will be happiest if she lives a life of humble service to the poorest of the poor, working long hours, giving up the conveniences of industrialized society, and having next to nothing that she can call her own. It seems misleading at best to say that her choice of this way of life is self-interested, for her conception of happiness involves forgetting about herself and devoting her attention to the needs of others. While we can say that it is in her interest to live out the kind of life she has chosen, we should be quick to add that her conception of happiness has taken her far beyond self-interest, for it is by renouncing her acquisitive self that she hopes to become a self whose attention is devoted to the needs of others.

THE PURSUIT OF SELF-INTEREST

Most people's thinking about their interest is superficial. When we think about what is good for us, we usually focus our attention on a relatively short span of time. Without concerted effort and practice, we are unlikely to see the significance of the present moment in the context of a major chunk of our lives, much less our life as a whole. But what we think important is altered when we view our activities in the context of what we want for a significant portion of our life. What might have seemed a gratifying diversion, becomes another part of a pattern of procrastination that is likely to delay graduation. What looked like an isolated case of working long hours to meet a deadline, is transformed when seen in the context of a habitual tendency to take the family for granted.

When we focus on the consequences of an individual act, we lose sight of the fact that many of our acts gain their significance in relation to patterns that take shape over extended periods of time. In isolation it might appear unimportant that I stretched the truth a little or spoke sharply to a subordinate; however, acts affect our lives not just as isolated units, but by reinforcing tendencies and patterns that are all but invisible except to a discerning eye looking from a sufficiently wide point of view.

So, in urging the use of self-interested thought only within the context of a conception of a desirable life, I have been trying to combat the tendency to allow our ideas of self-interest to be deformed by a bias for evaluating individual acts. Only by looking beyond the acts to policies we are following and the concerns and habits we are developing can we clarify our awareness of the direction our lives are moving. By thinking about how our activities are contributing to or undermining our efforts to have a quality life, we give our self-interested thinking the context it needs to work for us instead of against us.

In this larger context it may become apparent that following our desires does not always serve our interest. Sometimes we imagine that we can determine our interest by deciding what we desire most. But even if we deal with conflicting desires and long-range consequences, it is not clear that satisfying the desires we happen to have will give us the life we want. If our desires are formed by a consumer-oriented society, they may push us steadily toward the pursuit of more and more, without bringing us any closer to a satisfying life. To get beyond superficial thinking about our interests, we need to reflect on the desires we have and their place in the kind of life we want to lead. Doing so will often lead us to realize that our true interest lies in modifying what we want in accordance with some pattern of desirable living.

When the context in which we view our self-interest is sufficiently wide, we can recognize the importance of attending to the kind of self we are forming and how our various actions are contributing to or undermining a self capable of living the life we seek. Throughout this book I have called attention to a variety of factors relevant to self-formation that are important to consider in determining how to pursue self-interest. These have included:

- Developing habits and skills of self-control needed to effectively act for our good.
- Forming attachments to other people based on concern for their well-being.
- Internalizing limits which correspond to the self's concerns.
- Developing knowledge, skills, and interests needed for fulfilling one's talents, inclinations, and conception of what is worthwhile for a human being.

- Acquiring the concerns and skills needed for becoming engaged in meaningful or enjoyable activities.
- Modifying the self's concerns to harmonize with its ideals so that a unified identity may be achieved.

Forming the kind of self needed for a desirable life is a long-term project. It is easy to be distracted from pursuing this project by the pressures or incentives of the moment, but when we do so, we abandon the perspective required to give our self-interested thinking genuine coherence.

The pursuit of self-interest makes sense when it is placed in service of the kind of life one seeks to have. It becomes misguided when we imagine that we can determine our interest independently of thinking about our aspirations to have a particular kind of life and become the self such a life requires. Yet far too frequently people assume that they can effectively pursue their interest without attending to where the quest for particular benefits they desire is taking them. It is this truncated sort of self-interested thinking that leads to the sharpest kinds of conflict between self-interest and morality.

Whether or not self-interest conflicts with moral living depends on the nature of the self one aspires to be. I have tried to show throughout this book that a person might reasonably aspire to be a self whose identity is partially constituted by moral concerns and constraints. I have not tried to show that there is anything logically inconsistent with failing to form these aspirations. However, I have challenged the reader to think in sufficient depth about choosing a self to determine whether she can regard becoming a moral self as something essential or optional to her conception of a desirable life. The important question for an individual is not whether *someone* might reasonably choose to be an amoral self. It is whether *I*, given my best considered judgments about what is important or valuable or admirable, and my capacity for imaginative projection of possible alternatives, would be willing to become such a person.

Ultimately, the issue of what kind of self to be centers around what it takes to become a whole person whose reflective aspirations can be expressed in a particular way of life. Often, the only way to satisfy our aspirations is by incorporating into the self concerns for matters other than our own gratification. When we form this kind of self, it is appropriate to say that we have moved beyond self-interest. Or perhaps it would be better to say that our concern about our interest has assumed a more modest place in our motivational economy, a place that frees us to develop selves with greater depth. By breaking out of the tunnel vision that obsession with our interest can produce, we enlarge our vision of life's possibilities. By incorporating into our lives the full range of our aspirations, we give ourselves the opportunity to become whole persons with an identity that we have reflectively chosen to be our own.

Notes

INTRODUCTION: SELF-INTERESTED THINKING

[1]Søren Kierkegaard, *The Sickness Unto Death: A Christian Psychological Exposition For Upbuilding and Awakening*, trans. Howard V. Hong and Edna H. Hong (Princeton: Princeton University Press, 1980), 32-33.

[2]Robert Bellah, Richard Madsen, William Sullivan, Ann Swidler, and Stephen Tipton, *Habits of the Heart: Individualism and Commitment in American Life* (Berkeley: University of California Press, 1985), 290.

PRELUDE TO PART ONE

[1]David Schmidtz, *Rational Choice and Moral Agency* (Princeton: Princeton University Press, 1995), 108-9.

[2]James Griffin, *Well-Being: Its Meaning, Measurement and Moral Importance* (New York: Oxford University Press, 1986), 202.

CHAPTER ONE: THE DIFFICULTY OF SELF-INTERESTED BEHAVIOR

[1]Joseph Butler, *Five Sermons Preached At the Rolls Chapel and A Dissertation Upon the Nature of Virtue* (Indianapolis: The Bobbs-Merrill Company, 1950), 16.

[2]Søren Kierkegaard, *Either/Or*, Part II, trans. Howard Hong and Edna Hong, (Princeton: Princeton University Press, 1987), 207.

[3]Butler, 16.

[4]Michael Ryan, *Secret Life: An Autobiography* (New York: Vintage Books, 1995), 335.

[5]My discussion is indebted to Robert Roberts, "Will Power and the Virtues," *Philosophical Review* 93 (April, 1984): 227-247.

[6]Aristotle, *Nicomachean Ethics*, in *The Basic Works of Aristotle*, ed. Richard McKeon (New York: Random House, 1941), bk. II, ch. 1: 952-3.

[7]Harry Frankfurt, "Freedom of the Will and the Concept of a Person," *Journal of Philosophy*, 68 (1971): 5-20.

[8]I do not mean to deny here that rigidity can be undesirable. Rather I am exhibiting an either/or type of thinking which assumes only two possibilities: undisciplined or rigid.

[9]Albert Ellis and Robert A. Harper, *A New Guide to Rational Living* (No. Hollywood, California: Wilshire Book Company, 1975), 161.

CHAPTER TWO: THE RANGE OF HUMAN CONCERNS

[1]Francis Hutcheson, *An Inquiry Concerning Moral Good and Evil*, section II, in *British Moralists 1650-1800*, vol. I, ed. D. D. Raphael (Oxford: The Clarendon Press, 1969), 272.

[2]Charles Peirce, "The Fixation of Belief," in *Philosophical Writings of Peirce*, ed. Justus Buchler (New York: Dover Publications, Inc., 1940), 16.

[3]What I am calling universal egoism is usually called psychological egoism by philosophers. Good philosophical discussions of this idea may be found in Joel Feinberg, "Psychological Egoism," in *Reason and Responsibility: Readings in Some Basic Problems of Philosophy*, 9th ed., ed. Joel Feinberg (Belmont California: Wadsworth Publishing Company, 1996), 497-507, and in James Rachels, *The Elements of Moral Philosophy* (New York: Random House, 1986), 53-64. Both Feinberg and Rachels rely heavily, as I do, on arguments from Joseph Butler.

[4]Harry Browne, *How I Found Freedom in an Unfree World* (New York: The Macmillan Company, 1973), 48.

[5]*Ibid.*

[6]*Ibid., 49.*

[7]Whether action to achieve a personal benefit is self-interested depends on how we define "self-interested action." As chapter one makes clear, not all acts to achieve benefits are in fact in one's self-interest. However, this chapter explores the possibility of calling acts self-interested if they have a certain type of motive.

[8]I am following the approach to defining "psychological egoism" used by Gregory Kavka in *Hobbesian Moral and Political Theory* (Princeton: Princeton University Press, 1986), 35-44.

[9]A discussion of the range of psychological evidence for altruistic behavior may be found in Michael A. Wallach and Lise Wallach, *Psychology's Sanction for Selfishness: The Error of Egoism in Theory and Therapy* (San Francisco: W. H. Freeman and Company, 1983). This book shows how assumptions that humans are only selfishly motivated permeate discussions in both popular and academic psychology, leading to systematic misinterpretations of the evidence.

[10]Aristotle, *Nicomachean Ethics*, in *The Basic Works of Aristotle*, ed. Richard McKeon (New York: Random House, 1941), bk. II, ch. 3: 954.

[11]Charles Taylor argues for this position, using the concept of "strong evaluations." See his *Sources of the Self: The Making of Modern Identity* (Cambridge: Harvard University Press, 1989), 3-107.

[12]Samuel P. Olner and Pearl M. Olner, *The Altruistic Personality: Rescuers of Jews in Nazi Europe* (New York: The Free Press, 1988).

CHAPTER THREE: GETTING WHAT YOU WANT

[1]Oscar Wilde, *Lady Windermere's Fan* in *The Works of Oscar Wilde*, ed. G. F. Maine (New York: E. P. Dutton & Company, Inc., 1954), 402.

[2]John Stuart Mill, *The Autobiography of John Stuart Mill* (New York: Columbia University Press, 1924), 94.

[3]N. J. H. Dent, *The Moral Psychology of the Virtues* (Cambridge: Cambridge University Press, 1984), 96-119.

[4]James Griffin contrasts such global desires with more local ones in *Well-Being: Its Meaning, Measurement and Moral Importance* (Oxford: Oxford University Press, 1986). He argues that desires form a hierarchy with concerns at lower levels being taken into account at higher levels.

[5]Many philosophers have used similar thought experiments. See, for example, Robert Nozick's use of an experience machine in *Anarchy, State and Utopia* (New York: Basic Books, 1974), 42-45.

[6]Thomas E. Hill, Jr., "Self-Respect Reconsidered," in *Autonomy and Self-Respect* (New York: Cambridge University Press, 1991), 19-24.

CHAPTER FOUR: DEALING WITH WHAT YOU DON'T WANT

[1]Augustine, *Confessions*, trans. Henry Chadwick, (New York: Oxford University Press, 1991), IV (9): 59-60.

[2]Victor Frankl, *Man's Search For Meaning: An Introduction to Logotherapy*, trans. Ilse Lasch, (Boston: Beacon Press, 1959), 67. Subsequent references to Frankl in this chapter are to this edition.

[3]Epictetus, *The Encheiridion*, in *The Discourses As Reported by Arrian, the Manual, and Fragments*, vol. II, trans. W.A. Oldfather (Cambridge: Harvard University Press, 1967), #1: 483. Subsequent references in the chapter to Epictetus are to this edition.

[4]The term "invulnerablity" is used by Steven Luper in *Invulnerablity: On Securing Happiness* (Chicago: Open Court Publishing Company, 1996).

[5]John Stuart Mill, *Utilitarianism*, ed. George Sher (Indianapolis: Hackett Publishing Company, 1979), ch. II: 9.

[6]Plato, *Apology* in *Great Dialogues of Plato*, trans. W. H. D. Rouse (New York: New American Library, 1956), 41d: 446.

[7]Luper, 44-46.

[8]David G. Myers, *The Pursuit of Happiness: Discovering the Pathway to Fulfillment, Well-Being, and Enduring Personal Joy* (New York: Avon Books, 1992), 48.

PRELUDE TO PART TWO

[1]Lewis Carroll, *Alice's Adventures in Wonderland & Through The Looking Glass* (New York: New American Library Inc., 1960), 27.

[2]Søren Kierkegaard, *Either/Or*, Pt. II, eds. Howard V. Hong and Edna H. Hong (Princeton: Princeton University Press, 1987), 177.

CHAPTER FIVE: THE EXPANDED SELF

[1]John Stuart Mill, *Utilitarianism* (Indianapolis: Hackett Publishing Company, Inc., 1979), ch. II: 13.

[2]Henry Sidgwick, *The Methods of Ethics* (Chicago: University of Chicago Press, 1962), 501.

[3]Columbia Pictures Industries, Inc., 1993.

[4]Alfred Lord Tennyson, "In Memorium."

[5]Deal W. Hudson, *Happiness and the Limits of Satisfaction* (Lanham, Maryland: Rowman and Littlefield Publishers, Inc., 1996), xviii-xix.

[6]The unwillingness to trade is one of Mill's tests for superior kinds of pleasure. *Utilitarianism*, ch. II: 8.

[7]Mark Overvold has argued that accounts of self-interest in terms of personal utility or "what the agent most wants to do" can conflict with the possibility of self-sacrifice. See his "Self-Interest and the Concept of Self-sacrifice," *Canadian Journal of Philosophy*, X, 1 (March, 1980): 105-118. I agree that these kinds of accounts of self-interest are defective. The defect arises, I think, from attempting to view all motivation on a simple desire-satisfaction model. Acting on an altruistic desire can be in one's self-interest, but in some cases where such a desire conflicts significantly with nonaltruistic desires, it is implausible to call the motivation self-interested. We have something closer to motivation by an ideal than an attempt to maximize desire satisfaction.

[8]Jean Hampton, "Selflessness and the Loss of Self," in *Altruism*, eds. Ellen Frankel Paul, Fred D. Miller, Jr., and Jeffrey Paul (Cambridge: Cambridge University Press, 1993), 135-165.

[9]The issue of an individual's connection to a larger whole is explored in a different way in Chapter Eight (The Engaged Self).

CHAPTER 6: THE LIMITED SELF

[1]*The Republic of Plato*, trans. Francis Cornford (Oxford: Oxford University Press, 1945), bk. IX, 589d: 317.

[2]Gerald Postema, "Hume's Reply to the Sensible Knave," *History of Philosophy Quarterly* 5 (1988): 35.

[3]Søren Kierkegaard, *Either/Or*, Pt. II, eds. Howard V. Hong and Edna H. Hong (Princeton: Princeton University Press, 1987), 254.

[4]Orion Pictures Corporation, 1989.

[5]*Ibid.*

[6]Julia Annas, "The Good Life and the Good Lives of Others," in *The Good Life and the Human Good*, eds. Ellen Frankel Paul, Fred D. Miller Jr., and Jeffrey Paul (Cambridge: Cambridge University Press, 1992), 133-148.

[7]Dag Hammarskjöld, *Markings*, trans. Leif Sjobert & W. H. Auden (New York: Ballantine Books, 1964), 9.

[8]David Schmidtz, *Rational Choice and Moral Agency* (Princeton: Princeton University Press, 1995), 103f.

CHAPTER SEVEN: THE DEVELOPED SELF

[1]John Stuart Mill, *Utilitarianism* (Indianapolis: The Hackett Publishing Company, Inc., 1979), ch. II: 13-14.

[2]Robert Grudin, *Time and the Art of Living* (New York: The Houghton Mifflin Company, 1982), 41.

[3]Portions of this chapter are adapted from David Holley, "Self-Transforming Experiences," *The Personalist Forum* 13 (1997).

[4]Willy Russell, *Educating Rita* (New York: Samuel French Inc., 1981), 33-34.

[5]*Ibid.*, 12-13.

[6]*Ibid.*, 21.

[7]*Ibid.*, 32.

[8]Mill, 9.

[9]*Ibid.*

[10]Russell, 8.

[11]*Ibid., 48.*

[12]*Ibid., 48-49.*

[13]Grudin, 40.

[14]*Ibid.*

CHAPTER EIGHT: THE ENGAGED SELF

[1]Roy Baumeister, *Meanings of Life* (New York: The Guilford Press, 1991), 77.

[2]Peter Singer, *How Are We to Live?: Ethics in an Age of Self-Interest* (New York: Prometheus Books, 1995), 20.

[3]Mihaly Csikszentmihalyi, *Flow: The Psychology of Optimal Experience* (New York: Harper and Row, 1990), 2.

[4]Leo Tolstoy, *A Confession and Other Religious Writings* (New York: Penguin Books, 1987), 30.

[5]*Ibid.*

[6]*Ibid.*, 31.

[7]Thomas Nagel, "The Absurd," in *Mortal Questions* (Cambridge: Cambridge University Press, 1979), 11-23.

[8]Tolstoy, 32.

[9]It is possible to make an activity of this sort meaningful by connecting it with a purpose of some kind. For example, students might view what they are doing as a kind of competitive game. But giving the activity this sort of point may or may not be sufficient to make it worth doing from their point of view.

[10]Dan McAdams, *The Stories We Live By: Personal Myths and the Making of the Self* (New York: The Guilford Press, 1993).

[11]Anne Colby and William Damon, *Some Do Care: Contemporary Lives of Moral Commitment* (New York: The Free Press, 1992), 39-64.

[12]*Ibid.*, 47.

[13]*Ibid.*, 64

[14]*Ibid.*

[15]*Ibid.*, 59.

[16]Jeremy Bernstein, *The Life It Brings: One Physicist's Beginnings* (New York: Penguin Books, 1987), 170.

[17]David Hume, *An Enquiry Concerning the Principles of Morals* in *Hume's Ethical Writings*, ed. Alasdair MacIntyre (New York: The Macmillan Company, 1965), 60ff.

[18]Csikszentmihalyi, 4.

PRELUDE TO PART THREE

[1]Lewis Carroll, *Alice's Adventures in Wonderland & Through The Looking Glass* (New York: New American Library Inc., 1960), 47.

[2]Søren Kierkegaard, *Either/Or*, Part II, eds. Howard V. Hong and Edna H. Hong (Princeton: Princeton University Press, 1987), 259.

CHAPTER NINE: IDENTITY

[1]Charles Taylor, *Sources of the Self: The Making of Modern Identity* (Cambridge: Harvard University Press, 1989), 30.

[2]Aristotle, *Nicomachean Ethics*, in *The Basic Works of Aristotle*, ed. Richard McKeon (New York: Random House, 1941), bk. IX, ch. 8: 1087.

[3]Epictetus, *The Discourses As Reported By Arrian, The Manual, and the Fragments*, vol. I, trans. W.A. Oldfather (Cambridge: Harvard University Press), bk. II, ch. xxii: 399.

[4]Orian Pictures Company, 1983.

[5]William James, *The Principles of Psychology*, vol. 1 (Cambridge: Harvard University Press, 1981), 282.

[6]Harry Frankfurt, "On the Necessity of Ideals," in *The Moral Self*, eds. Gil G. Noam and Thomas E. Wren (Cambridge: The MIT Press, 1993), 24-25.

[7]Aristotle, bk. IX, ch. 8: 1086.

[8]*Ibid.*, 1087.

[9]*Ibid.*

[10]Anne Colby and William Damon, *Some Do Care: Contemporary Lives of Moral Commitment* (New York: The Free Press, 1992), 300.

[11]*Ibid., 299.*

[12]Marcus Aurelius, *The Meditations*, trans. G. M. A. Grube (New York: Hackett Publishing Company, 1983), III: 7.

CHAPTER TEN: INTEGRITY

[1]Herbert Fingarette, *Self-Deception* (New York: Humanities Press Inc., 1969), 87.

[2]Lynn McFall, "Integrity," in *Ethics and Personality: Essays in Moral Psychology*, ed. John Deigh (Chicago: University of Chicago Press, 1992), 94.

[3]Harry Frankfurt, "The Importance of What We Care About," in *The Importance of What We Care About* (Cambridge: Cambridge University Press, 1988), 86.

[4]My account of Sakharov is based on Anne Colby and William Damon, *Some Do Care: Contemporary Lives of Moral Commitment* (New York: The Free Press, 1992), 9-14.

[5]*Ibid.*, 13.

[6]Gabriele Taylor, "Shame, Integrity, and Self-Respect," in *Dignity, Character, and Self-Respect*, ed. Robin Dillon (New York: Routledge, 1995), 168.

[7]Stephen Carter, *Integrity* (New York: HarperCollins, 1996), 107-121.

[8]Robert Bolt, *A Man For All Seasons* (New York: Vintage Books, 1960), 81.

[9]*Ibid.*, xi.

[10]*Ibid.*, 71-72.

[11]*Ibid.*, 71.

[12]Frankfurt, 87.

CHAPTER 11: SELF-TRANSFORMATION

[1]John Kekes, *The Examined Life* (University Park, Pennsylvania: The Pennsylvania State University Press, 1992), 87-88.

[2]Jonathan Glover, *The Philosophy and Psychology of Personal Identity* (New York: Penguin Books, 1988), 132.

[3]David Schmidtz, *Rational Choice and Moral Agency* (Princeton: Princeton University Press, 1995), 102.

[4]David G. Myers, *The Pursuit of Happiness: Discovering the Pathway To Fulfillment, Well-Being, and Enduring Personal Joy* (New York: Avon Books, 1992), 123.

[5]William James, *The Principles of Psychology*, vol. I (Cambridge: Harvard University Press, 1981), 130-131.

[6]*Ibid.*, 131.

[7]Nathaniel Hawthorne, *The Centenary Edition of the Works of Nathaniel Hawthorne*, vol. XI *The Snow-Image and Uncollected Tales* (Columbus: Ohio State University Press, 1974), 48.

CONCLUSION: BEYOND SELF-INTEREST

[1]Whether this example is a case of a conflict between what I must do and my considered judgment of what is in my interest may depend on whether my conception of benefit gives priority to the benefit of maintaining a unified identity. However, as the next section makes clear, maintaining integrity is very different from any other kind of self-interested reason. One who is acting to maintain integrity is overriding any calculation of gains or loses. In cases of this sort where the agent is motivated to sacrificial action, the action is only self-interested if we imagine an agent who has advanced beyond self-interest enough to blur the lines between self-interest and other kinds of motivations.

Additional Reading

Annas Julia. *The Morality of Happiness*. Oxford: Oxford University Press, 1993.

Aristotle, *Nicomachean Ethics* in *The Basic Works of Aristotle*. Edited by Richard McKeon. New York: Random House, 1941.

Augustine. *Confessions*. Translated by Henry Chadwick. New York: Oxford University Press, 1991.

Aurelius, Marcus. *The Meditations*. Translated by G. M. A. Grube. New York: Hackett Publishing Company, 1983.

Baumeister, Roy. *Meanings of Life*. New York: The Guilford Press, 1991.

Bellah, Robert, Richard Madsen, William Sullivan, Ann Swidler, and Stephen Tipton. *Habits of the Heart: Individualism and Commitment in American Life*. Berkeley: University of California Press, 1985.

Bernstein, Jeremy. *The Life It Brings: One Physicist's Beginnings*. New York: Penguin Books, 1987.

Blustein, Jeffrey. *Caring and Commitment: Taking the Personal Point of View*. Oxford: Oxford University Press, 1991.

Bolt, Robert. *A Man For All Seasons*. New York: Vintage Books, 1960.

Brinthaupt. Thomas M. and Richard Lipka. *Changing the Self: Philosophies, Techniques, and Experiences*. Albany: State University of New York Press, 1994.

________. *The Self: Definitional and Methodological Issues*. Albany: State University of New York Press, 1992.

Browne, Harry, *How I Found Freedom in an Unfree World*. New York: The Macmillan Company, 1973.

Buchler, Justus. *The Philosophical Writings of Charles Peirce*. New York: Dover Publications, Inc., 1940.

Butler, Joseph. *Five Sermons Preached At the Rolls Chapel and A Dissertation Upon the Nature of Virtue*. Indianapolis: The Bobbs-Merrill Company, 1950.

Carter, Stephen L. *Integrity*. New York: Basic Books, 1996.

Colby, Anne and William Damon. *Some Do Care: Contemporary Lives of Moral Commitment*. New York: The Free Press, 1992.

Csikszentmihalyi, Mihaly. *Flow: The Psychology of Optimal Experience*. New York: Harper and Row, 1990.

Deigh, John, ed. *Ethics and Personality: Essays in Moral Psychology*. Chicago: University of Chicago Press, 1992.

Dent, N. J. H. *The Moral Psychology of the Virtues*. Cambridge: Cambridge University Press, 1984.

Dillon, Robin. *Dignity, Character, and Self-Respect*. New York: Routledge, 1995.

Ellis Albert, and Robert A. Harper. *A New Guide to Rational Living*. No. Hollywood, California: Wilshire Book Company, 1975.

Epictetus. *The Discourses As Reported by Arrian, the Manual, and Fragments*. Translated by W. A. Oldfather. Cambridge: Harvard University Press, 1967.

Feinberg, Joel, "Psychological Egoism," in *Reason and Responsibility: Readings in Some Basic Problems of Philosophy*, 9th ed. Edited by Joel Feinberg. Belmont, California: Wadsworth Publishing Company, 1996.

Fingarette, Herbert. *Self-Deception*. New York: Humanities Press Inc., 1969.

Frankfurt, Harry. "Freedom of the Will and the Concept of a Person." *Journal of Philosophy* 68 (1971): 5-20.

________. *The Importance of What We Care About*. Cambridge: Cambridge University Press, 1988.

Frankl, Victor. *Man's Search For Meaning: An Introduction to Logotherapy*. Translated by Ilse Lasch. Boston: Beacon Press, 1959.

Gauthier, David P., ed. *Morality and Rational Self-Interest*. Englewood Cliffs, New Jersey: Prentice-Hall, Inc., 1970.

Glover, Jonathan. *The Philosophy and Psychology of Personal Identity*. New York: Penguin Books, 1988.

Griffin, James. *Well-Being: Its Meaning, Measurement and Moral Importance*. Oxford: Oxford University Press, 1986.

Grudin, Robert. *Time and the Art of Living*. New York: The Houghton Mifflin Company, 1982.

Hammarskjöld, Dag. *Markings*. Translated by Leif Sjobert & W. H. Auden. New York: Ballantine Books, 1964.

Hawthorne, Nathaniel. *The Centenary Edition of the Works of Nathaniel Hawthorne*, vol. XI, *The Snow-Image and Uncollected Tales*. Columbus: Ohio State University Press, 1974.

Heil, John, ed. *Rationality, Morality and Self-Interest: Essays Honoring Mark Carl Overvold*. Lanham, Maryland: Rowman & Littlefield Publishers, Inc., 1993.

Helm, Bennett. "Integration and Fragmentation of the Self." *The South-*

ern Journal of Philosophy XXXIV (1996): 43-63.

Hill, Thomas. *Autonomy and Self-Respect.* New York: Cambridge University Press, 1991.

Hudson, Deal W. *Happiness and the Limits of Satisfaction.* Lanham Maryland: Rowman & Littlefield Publishers, Inc., 1996.

Hume, David. *Hume's Ethical Writings.* Edited by Alasdair MacIntyre. New York: The Macmillan Company, 1965.

James, William. *The Principles of Psychology*, 2 vols. Cambridge: Harvard University Press, 1981.

Kavka, Gregory. *Hobbsian Moral and Political Theory.* Princeton: Princeton University Press, 1986.

Kekes, John. *The Examined Life.* University Park, Pennsylvania: The Pennsylvania State University Press, 1992.

________. *Moral Wisdom and Good Lives.* Ithaca: Cornell University Press, 1995.

Kierkegaard, Søren. *Either/Or*, 2 vols. Translated by Howard Hong and Edna Hong. Princeton: Princeton University Press, 1987.

________. *The Sickness Unto Death: A Christian Psychological Exposition For Upbuilding and Awakening.* Translated by Howard Hong and Edna Hong. Princeton: Princeton University Press, 1980.

Kruschwitz, Robert B. and Robert C. Roberts, eds. *The Virtues: Contemporary Essays on Moral Character.* Belmont, California: Wadsworth Publishing Company, 1987.

Luper, Steven. *Invulnerability: On Securing Happiness.* Chicago: Open Court Publishing Company, 1996.

Mansbridge, Jane J., ed. *Beyond Self-Interest.* Chicago: University of Chicago Press, 1990.

Martin, Mike W. *Self-Deception and Morality.* Lawrence, Kansas: University Press of Kansas, 1986.

________, ed. *Self-Deception and Self Understanding: New Essays in Philosophy and Psychology.* Lawrence, Kansas: University Press of Kansas, 1985.

McAdams, Dan. *The Stories We Live By: Personal Myths and the Making of the Self.* New York: The Guilford Press, 1993.

McFall, Lynne. "Happiness, Rationality, and Individual Ideals." *Review of Metaphysics* 38 (1984): 595-613.

Mill, John Stuart. *The Autobiography of John Stuart Mill.* New York: Columbia University Press, 1924.

________. *Utilitarianism.* Edited by George Sher. Indianapolis: Hackett Publishing Company, 1979.

Monroe, Kristen Renwick. *The Heart of Altruism: Perceptions of a Common Humanity*. Princeton: Princeton University Press, 1996.

Myers, David G. *The Pursuit of Happiness: Discovering the Pathway To Fulfillment, Well-Being, and Enduring Personal Joy*. New York: Avon Books, 1992.

Nagel, Thomas. *Mortal Questions*. Cambridge: Cambridge University Press, 1979.

________. *The Possibility of Altruism*. Princeton: Princeton University Press, 1970.

Noam, Gil and Thomas Wren, eds. *The Moral Self*. Cambridge: MIT Press, 1993.

Nozick Robert. *Anarchy, State and Utopia*. New York: Basic Books, 1974.

Nussbaum, Martha. *The Therapy of Desire: Theory and Practice in Hellenistic Ethics*. Princeton: Princeton University Press, 1994.

Olner, Samuel P. and Pearl M. Olner. *The Altruistic Personality: Rescuers of Jews in Nazi Europe*. New York: The Free Press, 1988.

Osterberg, Jan. *Self and Others: A Study of Ethical Egoism*. Boston: Kluwer Academic Publishers, 1988.

Overvold, Mark. "Self Interest and the Concept of Self-Sacrifice." *Canadian Journal of Philosophy* X (1980): 105-118.

Paul, Ellen Frankel, Fred D. Miller, Jr., and Jeffrey Paul, eds. *Altruism*. Cambridge: Cambridge University Press, 1993.

________. *The Good Life and the Human Good*. Cambridge: Cambridge University Press, 1992.

________. *Self-Interest*. Cambridge: Cambridge University Press, 1997.

Plato. *Great Dialogues of Plato*. Translated by W. H. D. Rouse. New York: New American Library, 1956.

Postema, Gerald. "Hume's Reply to the Sensible Knave." *History of Philosophy Quarterly* 5 (1988): 23-40.

Rachels, James. *The Elements of Moral Philosophy*. New York: Random House, 1986.

Rand, Ayn. *The Virtue of Selfishness*. New York: Penguin Books, 1961.

Raphael, D. D., ed. *British Moralists 1650-1800*. Oxford: The Clarendon Press, 1969.

Richardson, Henry. *Practical Reasoning About Final Ends*. Cambridge: Cambridge University Press, 1994.

Roberts, Robert. "Will Power and the Virtues." *Philosophical Review* 93 (1984): 227-247.

Rogers, Kelly, ed. *Self-Interest: An Anthology of Philosophical Perspectives*. New York: Routledge, 1997.

Russell, Willy. *Educating Rita*. New York: Samuel French Inc., 1981.

Ryan, Michael, *Secret Life: An Autobiography*. New York: Vintage Books, 1995.

Schmidtz, David. *Rational Choice and Moral Agency*. Princeton: Princeton University Press, 1995.

Sidgwick, Henry. *The Methods of Ethics*. Chicago: University of Chicago Press, 1962.

Singer, Irving. *The Creation of Value*. Baltimore: The Johns Hopkins University Press, 1992.

Singer, Peter. *How Are We to Live? Ethics in an Age of Self-Interest*. New York: Prometheus Books, 1995.

Taylor, Charles. *Sources of the Self: The Making of Modern Identity*. Cambridge: Harvard University Press, 1989.

Tolstoy, Leo. *A Confession and Other Religious Writings*. New York: Penguin Books, 1987.

Van Ingen, John. *Why Be Moral? The Egoistic Challenge*. New York: Peter Lang, 1994.

Wallach, Michael A. and Lise Wallach, *Psychology's Sanction for Selfishness: The Error of Egoism in Theory and Therapy*. San Francisco: W. H. Freeman and Company, 1983.

Wuthnow, Robert. *Learning To Care: Elementary Kindness in an Age of Indifference*. Oxford: Oxford University Press, 1995.

Index